Refutation of Helvetius

Denis Diderot
1758

NEWCOMB LIVRARIA
-PRESS-

Contents

Refutation of Helvétius

Reflections on the Book of the Mind by M. Helvetius

No work has made so much noise. The subject matter and the author's name have contributed to it. The author has been working on it for fifteen years; it is seven or eight years since he left his position as farmer-general to take the wife he has, and devote himself to the study of letters and philosophy. He lives for six months of the year in the country, secluded with a small number of people whom he has attached to himself; and he has a very pleasant house in Paris. What is certain is that it is up to him to be happy; for he has friends, a charming wife, sense, wit, consideration in this world, fortune, health and cheerfulness... The fools, the envious and the bigots must have risen up against his principles; and that's a lot of people... The object of his work is to consider the human mind from different angles, and to rely everywhere on facts. First, he deals with the human mind in itself. He then considers it in relation to truth and error... He seems to attribute sentience to matter in general; a system that is highly suitable for philosophers, and against which the superstitious cannot rise without running into great difficulties. There can be little doubt that animals feel, and that sentience in them is either a property of matter, or a quality of a spiritual substance. The superstitious dare not admit to either... The author of L'Esprit reduces all intellectual functions to sensibility. To perceive or to feel is the same thing, according to him. To judge or to feel is the same thing... He recognizes no difference between man and beast, except that of organization. So, lengthen a man's muzzle; make his nose, eyes, teeth and ears look like a dog's; cover him with hair; put him on all fours; and this man, even if he is a doctor from the Sorbonne, thus metamorphosed, will perform all the functions of a dog; he will bark, instead of arguing; he will gnaw bones, instead of solving sophisms; his main activity will be to smell; he will have almost all his soul in his nose; and he will follow a rabbit or a hare, instead of fanning an atheist or a heretic... On the other hand, take a dog; raise him up on his hind legs, round off his head, shorten his muzzle, remove his hair and tail, and you'll turn him into a doctor, pondering deeply on the mysteries of predestination and grace... If we consider that a man differs from another man only in organization, and differs from himself only in the variety that occurs in the organs; if we see him stammering in childhood, reasoning in middle age, and stammering again in old age; what he is in the state of health and sickness, tranquility and passion, we will not be far from this system... By considering the mind in relation to error and truth, M. Helvétius convinces himself that there is no such thing as a false mind. He attributes all our erroneous judgments to ignorance, the misuse of words and the ardor of passions... If a man reasons badly, it's because he doesn't have the data to reason better. He has not considered the object from every angle. The author applies this principle to luxury, about which so much has been written both for and against. He shows that those who defended it were right, and that those who attacked it were also right in what they said. But neither came to a comparison of advantages and disadvantages, and could not form a result, for lack of knowledge. M. Helvétius resolves this great question, and it is one of the most beautiful parts of his book... What he says about the abuse of words is superficial, but pleasant. In general, it is the main character of the book, to be pleasant to read in the driest matters, because it is sown with an infinity of historical traits that relieve. The author applies the abuse of words to matter, time and space. He's very short and tight here, and it's not hard to guess why. He applies what he thinks of the errors of passion to the spirit of conquest and the love of reputation; and by reasoning with two men whose judgment has been clouded by these two passions, he shows how passions lead us astray in general. This chapter is also crammed with pleasant anecdotes, and other bold and vigorous lines. There is a certain Egyptian priest who very eloquently reproaches some unbelievers for seeing in the Apis ox only an ox; and this priest resembles many others... That, in a nutshell, is the object and subject of the first discourse. It has three others, which we will discuss later.

After considering the spirit in itself, M. Helvétius considers it in relation to society. According to him, the general interest is the measure of our esteem for the mind, not the difficulty of the object or the extent of the enlightenment. He could cite a striking example. Let a geometer place three points on his paper; let him suppose that these three points attract each other in the inverse ratio of the square of the distances, and let him then seek the movement and the trace of these three points. Once this problem has been solved, he will read it out at a few Academy sessions: he will be listened to; his solution will be printed in a collection, where it will be confused with a thousand others, and forgotten; and it will scarcely be mentioned in the world, or among scholars. But if these three points come to represent the three principal bodies of nature; if one is called the earth, the other the moon, and the third the sun; then the solution to the three-point problem will represent the law of celestial bodies: the geometer will be called Newton; and his memory will live forever among men. However, whether the three points are just three points, or whether these three points represent three celestial bodies, the sagacity is the same, but the interest is quite different, and so is public consideration. The same applies to probity. The author considers it in itself, or in relation to an individual, a small company, a nation, different centuries, different countries, and the entire universe. In all these relationships, interest is always the measure of the case. It is even this interest that constitutes it: so that the author admits neither justice nor absolute injustice. This is his second paradox... This paradox is false in itself, and dangerous to establish: false because it is possible to find in our natural needs, in our life, in our existence, in our organization and sensibility that expose us to pain, an eternal basis for justice and injustice, whose general and particular interest then varies the notion in a hundred thousand different ways. It is, in truth, general and particular interest that metamorphoses the idea of just and unjust; but its essence is independent of it. What seems to have misled our author is that he stuck to the facts that showed him just or unjust in a hundred thousand opposite forms, and that he closed his eyes to the nature of man, where he would have recognized its foundations and origin... He does not seem to me to have had an exact idea of what is meant by probity relative to the whole universe. He turned it into an empty word: which would not have happened to him, if he had considered that, wherever in the world it may be, he who gives drink to the thirsty and food to the hungry is a good man; and that probity relative to the universe is nothing other than a feeling of benevolence which embraces the human race in general; a feeling which is neither false nor chimerical... This is the subject and analysis of the speech, in which the author occasionally raises a number of important questions, such as true and false virtues, good taste, good manners, moralists and hypocritical moralists, the importance of morality and the means of perfecting it.

The subject of his third discourse is the mind, considered either as a gift of nature, or as an effect of education. Here, the author sets out to show that, of all the causes by which men can differ from one another, organization is the least; so that there is no man in whom passion, interest, education and chance could not have overcome the obstacles of nature, and made him a great man ; nor is there a great man in whom the lack of passion, interest, education and certain hazards could not have made him stupid, despite the most fortunate organization. This is his third paradox. Credat judæus Apella... The author is obliged here to appreciate all the qualities of the soul, considered in one man in relation to another; which he does with great sagacity: and however reluctant one may be to receive a paradox as strange as his, one does not read it without feeling shaken... The fallacy of this whole discourse seems to me to lie in several causes, of which here are the main ones: 1° the author does not know, or seems unaware of, the prodigious difference there is between effects (however slight the difference between causes), when causes act for a long time and without ceasing; 2° he has not considered either the variety of characters, one cold, the other slow; one sad, the other melancholy, cheerful, etc.. In a word, how much he differs from himself in a thousand circumstances where the slightest disturbance in organization occurs. A slight alteration in the brain reduces a man of genius to a state of imbecility. What will he do with this man, if the alteration, instead of being accidental and transitory, is natural? 3° He has not seen that, having made all the difference between man and beast consist in organization, it would be contradictory not to also make all the difference between man of genius and ordinary man consist in the same cause. In a word, the whole of the third speech seems to me to be a false calculation, in which neither all the elements, nor the elements we have employed, have been given their proper value. We have failed to see the insurmountable barrier that separates the man whom nature has destined for some function, from the man who brings to it only work, interest, attention, passions... This discourse, false in substance, is filled with beautiful details on the origin of passions, on their energy, on avarice, ambition, pride, friendship, etc... The author advances, in the same discourse, on the goal of passions, a fourth paradox; it is that physical pleasure is the last object they propose to themselves; which I believe to be false again. How many men, after having exhausted in their youth all the physical happiness that can be expected from the passions, become some avaricious, others ambitious, others lovers of glory! Will it be said that they have in view, in their new passion, those very goods from which they are disgusted?.. From wit, probity and passions, M. Helvétius moves on to what these qualities become under different governments, and especially under despotism. All the author needed was to see despotism as a beast hideous enough to give these chapters more color and force. Although full of bold truths, they are a little languid.

M. Helvétius' fourth discourse considers the mind in its various aspects: it is either genius, or sentiment, or imagination, or the mind proper, or the fine mind, or the strong mind, or the beautiful mind, or taste, or the just mind, or the spirit of society, or the spirit of conduct, or common sense, and so on. It is easy to see that the basis of this work is laid on four great paradoxes... Sensibility is a general property of matter. To perceive, reason and judge is to feel: the first paradox... There is neither justice nor absolute injustice. The general interest is the measure of the esteem of talents, and the essence of virtue: second paradox... It is education, not organization, that makes men different; and men come from the hands of nature, all almost equally suited to everything: third paradox... The last goal of passions is physical goods: fourth paradox... Add to this fund an incredible multitude of things on public worship, morals and government; on man, legislation and education; and you will know the whole matter of this work. It is very methodical; and this is one of its main faults: firstly, because method, when it is of apparatus, cools, weighs down and slows down; secondly, because it takes away from everything the air of freedom and genius; thirdly, because it has the appearance of argumentation; fourthly, and this reason is particular to the work, it is that there is nothing that wants to be proved with less affectation, more stealthy, less announced than a paradox. A paradoxical author must never say his word, but always his proof: he must enter his reader's soul by stealth, and not by force. This is the great art of Montaigne, who never wants to prove, but always goes about proving, and tossing me from white to black, and black to white. Besides, the apparatus of the method is like the scaffold that is always left standing after the building has been erected. It's a necessary thing to work on, but it's not something to be seen when the work is finished. It marks a mind that is too quiet, too in control of itself. The spirit of invention is restless, moving, stirring in an unregulated way; it seeks. The spirit of method arranges, orders, and assumes that everything has been found... This is the main flaw in this work. If everything the author has written had been piled up like a jumble, if there had only been a muted order in the author's mind, his book would have been infinitely more pleasant, and, without seeming so, infinitely more dangerous... Add to this the fact that it is full of stories: Now, storytelling fits perfectly in the mouth and in the writing of a man who seems to have no goal, and to wander and niggle; instead of these storytelling being only particular facts, one requires from the methodical author reasons in abundance and facts with sobriety... Among the facts spread in the book of the Spirit, there are some of bad taste and bad choice. I say the same of the notes. In this, a strict friend would have done the author a great service. With a stroke of the pen, he would have removed everything that displeases... There are truths in this work that upset man, announced too bluntly... There are expressions that are commonly taken the wrong way in the world, and to which the author gives, without warning, a different meaning. He should have avoided this inconvenience... There are important chapters, which are merely sketched... Ten years ago, this work would have been brand new; but today the philosophical spirit has made so much progress, that we find few new things in it... It is properly the preface to the Esprit des lois, although the author does not always agree with Montesquieu... It is inconceivable that this book, made expressly for the nation, for everywhere it is clear, everywhere amusing, everywhere having charm, women appearing everywhere as the author's idols, being properly the plea of subordinates against their superiors, appearing in a time when all the trampled orders are quite discontented, when the spirit of sling is more fashionable than ever, when the government is neither excessively loved, nor prodigiously esteemed; it is quite astonishing that, in spite of this, it has revolted almost all minds. It's a paradox that needs explaining... The style of this work is as colorful as a rainbow: playful, poetic, severe, sublime, light, elevated, ingenious, grand, dazzling, whatever pleases the author and the subject... Let's summarize. The Book of the Mind is the work of a man of merit. It contains many general principles that are false; but, on the other hand, it contains an infinite number of detailed truths. The author has raised metaphysics and morality to a high pitch; and any writer who wishes to treat the same subject, and who respects himself, will look closely at it. The ornaments are small for the building. Things of the imagination are overdone: there is nothing so fond of the sloppy and disheveled as the thing imagined. The general clamor against this work perhaps shows how many hypocrites of probity there are. Often the author's proofs are too weak, considering the strength of the assertions; the assertions being especially clearly and plainly stated. All in all, it's a furious blow to prejudices of all kinds. This book will be useful to men. It will subsequently bring the author into esteem; and although it lacks the genius that characterizes Montesquieu's Esprit des lois, and reigns in Buffon's Histoire naturelle, it will nonetheless be counted among the great books of the century.

REFUTATION FOLLOWED OF HELVÉTIUS' WORK INTITLED

"THE MAN"

FIRST VOLUME

PREFACE

Page 1. - If I had given this book during my lifetime, I would have exposed myself to persecution, and would have accumulated neither riches nor new dignities.

We shall see later how contrary this admission is to the author's principles. And why would he have given it?

Page 10 - The (French) nation is today the scorn of Europe. No salutary crisis will give it back its freedom; it will perish through consumption. Conquest is the only remedy for its misfortunes, and the effectiveness of such a remedy depends on chance and circumstance.

Current experience proves the contrary. Let the honest people who now occupy the highest positions in the State keep them only for ten years, and all our misfortunes will be repaired.

The re-establishment of the old magistracy has brought back the time of freedom.

We have long seen the arms of man struggle against the arms of nature; but the arms of man tire, and the arms of nature never tire.

A kingdom such as this can be compared to a huge bell set in flight. A long succession of imbecile children tie themselves to the rope, and make every effort to stop the bell, whose oscillations they successively diminish; but sooner or later a vigorous arm comes along and restores all its movement.

Under any government, nature has set limits to the misfortune of peoples. Beyond these limits, it's either death, flight or revolt. The land must be given back a portion of the wealth it yields; the farmer and landowner must live. This order of things is eternal, and the most inept and ferocious despot cannot violate it.

I wrote before the death of Louis XV: "This preface is bold: the author bluntly declares that our ills are incurable. And perhaps I would have agreed with him, had the reigning monarch been young.

Someone once asked how to restore morals to a corrupt people. I replied: As Medea restored youth to her father, by skinning and boiling him..... Then, this answer would not have been very out of place.

SECTION I.

The author employs the fifteen chapters that make up this section to establish his favorite paradox, "that education alone makes all the difference between roughly well-organized individuals....." a condition into which he brings neither strength, nor weakness, nor health, nor disease, nor any of those physical or moral qualities that diversify temperaments and characters.

CHAPTER I.

Page 2. - I have looked upon wit, genius and virtue as the product of instruction.

- Alone?

- This idea always seems true to me.

- It is false, and it is for this reason that it will never be sufficiently proven.

- I've been told that education has a greater influence on the genius and character of men and peoples than we might have thought.

- And that's all we could give you.

Page 4. - If organization is what makes us what we are, why blame the teacher for the ignorance and stupidity of his pupils?

I know of no system more consoling for parents and more encouraging for teachers. That's its advantage.

But I know of no system more distressing for children who are thought to be equally suited to everything; no system more capable of fulfilling the conditions of a society of mediocre men, and of leading astray the genius who does only one thing well; nor any system more dangerous because of the obstinacy it must inspire in superiors who, after having applied a class of pupils for a long time and without success to objects for which they had no natural inclination, will reject them into the world where they will no longer be good for anything. You don't give a greyhound a nose, you don't give a hound the speed of a greyhound; no matter what you do, this one will keep his nose, and that one will keep his legs.

CHAPTER II.

Page 5. - Man is born ignorant, not stupid; and it is not even without difficulty that he becomes so.

It is almost the opposite that should have been said. Man is always born ignorant, and very often foolish; and when he is not, nothing is easier than to make him so, nor, unfortunately, anything more consistent with experience.

Stupidity and genius occupy the two extremes of the human mind. It's impossible to move stupidity; it's easy to move genius.

Page 6. - There are two kinds of stupidity: one natural, the other acquired.

I'd like to know how to overcome natural stupidity. All men are classified between the greatest possible penetration and the most complete stupidity: between M. d'Alembert and M. d'Outrelot; and in spite of all institutions, each remains more or less on his own rung. Allow me to feel a man out, and I'll soon be able to discern what comes from application and what comes from nature. He who lacks this tact will often mistake the instrument for the work, and the work for the instrument.

There's a small step between each rung that's impossible to surmount, and to compensate for natural inequality, you need stubborn work on one side, and almost as continuous neglect on the other.

The man whom nature has placed on his rung stands firm and effortless. The man who has jumped onto a rung higher than the one he held from nature, staggers there, is always uncomfortable; he ponders deeply the problem that the other solves while he is tied up with bunting.

Here the author confuses stupidity with ignorance.

Page 7. - Once the mind has been burdened with the weight of learned ignorance, it no longer rises to the truth; it has lost the tendency that carried it towards it.....

And is this natural or acquired tendency the same in everyone?

The man who knows nothing can learn; it's just a question of igniting the desire within him.

And is everyone equally susceptible to this desire?

Page 8. - What does a teacher do? What does he desire? To spread the wings of genius.

So there is genius prior to the institution.

The ancients will retain a superiority over the moderns in morals, politics and legislation that they owe not to organization, but to institution.

And what does this prove?

- That one nation differs little from another.

- Who can deny it?

- That the French, raised like the Romans, would also have their Caesar, their Scipio, their Pompey, their Cicero.

- Why not? So, whatever the nation, a good education would make a great man, an Annibal, an Alexander, an Achilles, out of a Thersite, out of any individual! Convince anyone of this, but not me.

Why are such illustrious names so rare in those very nations where all citizens received the education you advocate?

Monsieur Helvétius, a quick question: here are five hundred children who have just been born; we're going to give them up to you to be raised at your discretion; tell me, how many men of genius will you give us back? Why not five hundred? Squeeze all your answers together, and you'll find that in the final analysis they all boil down to differences in organization, the primal source of laziness, thoughtlessness, stubbornness and other vices and passions.

Page 12 - The true preceptors of our childhood are the objects that surround us.

- True enough: but how do they teach us?

- Through sensation.

- But is it possible that, while organization is different, sensation is the same?

Such is its diversity, that if each individual could create for himself a language analogous to what he is, there would be as many languages as there are individuals; one man would say neither hello nor goodbye like another.

- But would there then be no truth, goodness or beauty?

- I don't think so; the variety of these idioms would not be enough to alter these ideas.

CHAPTER III.

Page 13. - The more painful the falls, the more instructive they are...

- I agree. But are there any two children in the world for whom the same fall was equally painful, in general, for whom any sensation could be identical? This is the first insurmountable barrier between their progress; and where does this barrier lie? In the organization. One of them lies on the ground and cries out: "I'm dead! The other gets up without a word, shakes himself off, and walks away.

There are certain actions of childhood where a man's entire destiny is written. Alcibiades and Cato repeated two words from their early years all their lives: Gare toi-même... Lâche... If Helvétius had weighed up these expressions of character, prior to any education, from the age of the jaquette and the jacks, he would have felt that it is nature that makes these children, and not the lesson. The art of converting lead into gold is a less ridiculous alchemy than that of making a Regulus out of the first person who comes along. All these lines by the author are nothing but projection powder.

Page 15 - Two brothers travel, one over steep mountains, the other through flower-filled valleys. On their return, they talk about what they have seen, and an exchange of sensations takes place between them. The image of nature's horror passes from the head of one to the brain of the other; and the former becomes intoxicated by the painting of its charms. One wants to go and shudder at the sight of abysses, at the crash of torrents: the other to lie down softly on the tender grass and fall asleep to the murmur of streams. This is because one is brave, and his brother is voluptuous. Don't upset these natural inclinations, you'll only make two mediocre subjects.

CHAPTER IV.

Page 17. - A child is locked in a room, he is alone; he sees flowers, he considers them...

I agree. But another child, variously born, will either fall asleep if he's a coward, or mutter between his teeth abusive words against his father or teacher, if he's vindictive. Cowardly or vindictive, he won't even know if there was a pot of flowers next to him.

CHAPTER V.

Page 18. - Ideas dependent on character...

- Monsieur Helvétius, are you listening? And isn't character an effect of organization?

CHAPTER VI.

Page 19 - Two brothers brought up in their parents' home have the same tutor, see more or less the same objects and read the same books. Age is the only difference that seems likely to affect their education. Do we want to make it null? Do we assume two twin brothers for this purpose? So be it. But will they have had the same nurse? How can we doubt the influence of the nanny's character on that of the infant?

No, Monsieur Helvétius, no, it doesn't matter, because, according to you, education fixes everything. Let's try to get along. You would be right if you agreed that, since the diversity of the first food affects the organization, there is no remedy; but this is not your opinion.

Page 20 - In the career of the sciences and the arts, which both initially traversed with equal step, if the first is stopped by some illness, if he lets the second take too much advance on him, study becomes odious to him.

If the first is stopped by some illness? And is there one more constant, more incurable than weakness or some other defect of organization?

What if he lets himself get too far ahead? And aren't some children naturally advanced or retarded?

And is nothing more discouraging for a child than to make up by work for the facility he lacks? And isn't it then that punishment is unjust, and often even impotent?

Page ibid - It is emulation that creates genius, and it is the desire to distinguish oneself that creates talent.

My dear philosopher, don't say that; but say that it's the causes that make them flourish, and no one will contradict you.

Emulation and desire don't put genius where it doesn't belong.

There are a thousand things that I find so far beyond my strength, that the hope of a throne, the very desire to save my life, would not make me attempt them; and what I say in this moment, there is not a single moment of my existence where I have not felt and thought it.

CHAPTER VII.

Page 22. - Chance has the greatest share in the formation of character.

But at the age of three, a child is sneaky, sad or cheerful, quick or slow; stubborn, impatient, angry, etc.; and for the rest of his life, chance would constantly present itself with a fork, that it would push nature away without reforming it: Naturam expellas furcâ, tamen usque recurret.

Page 23. - The sharpest characters are sometimes the product of an infinite number of small accidents.

It is a great mistake to take a man's conduct, even his habitual conduct, for his character.

We are naturally cowardly, we have the tone and bearing of a brave man; but are we brave for that?

We're naturally angry, but circumstances, the decorum of the state, interest dictate patience, we restrain ourselves; are we patient for that?

Borrowed traits are sharper than natural ones.

Ask the doctor, and he'll tell you that the character we have is not always the character we show, and that the former is the product of stiff or soft fiber, sweet or burning blood, thick or fluid lymph, acrid or soapy bile, and the state of the hard or fluid parts of our machine. Is your child voluptuous? Make him chase you all day, and make him drink a decoction of water-lily in the evening; it will be better than a chapter of Seneca.

Helvétius said earlier: If organization makes us almost entirely what we are, what right do we have to reproach the master for the stupidity of his pupil?

When he says here that chance has the greatest part in the formation of character, doesn't he see that his reasoning can be countered by saying: "If chance has the greatest part in the formation of our character, what right is there to reproach the master for the wickedness of his pupil?"

To propose to show education as the only difference between minds, the only basis for genius, talent and virtue; then to leave to chance the success of education and the formation of character: it seems to me that this is to reduce everything to nothing, and at the same time to satirize and glorify teachers.

CHAPTER VIII.

Give me Vaucanson's mother, and I won't make him an automaton flautist either. Send me into exile, or lock me up for ten years in the Bastille, and I won't come out with Paradise Lost in my hand. Pull me out of a wool merchant's store, enroll me in an acting troupe, and I'll compose neither Hamlet, nor King Lear, nor Tartuffe, nor Les Femmes Savantes, and my grandfather with his plût à Dieu will have said nothing but nonsense. I was more in love than Corneille, I also wrote verses for the woman I loved; but I didn't write the Cid or Rodogune. Yes, Monsieur Helvétius, you will be objected that such fortunes only produce such effects on men organized in a certain way, and you will not reply to this objection.

These coincidences are like the spark that ignites a barrel of spirits, or is extinguished in a tub of water.

Page 26. - Genius can only be the product of strong attention... (and page 27)

Genius is a product of chance.

These are strange assertions. I'd gnaw my fingers to the bone if genius didn't come to me. I can dream of all the happy coincidences that could give me genius, but I can't think of any.

But let's grant the author that with strong, concentrated attention to a single important object, one will acquire genius. You'll see that, however organized you are, you're a master at applying yourself strongly! There are men, and there are many of them, who are incapable of long, violent mental restraint. All their lives, they are what Newton, Leibnitz and Helvétius sometimes were. What can we do with these people? Clerks.

Page ibid. - The only disposition that man brings to science at birth is the ability to compare and combine.

Fair enough. But is this faculty the same in all individuals? If it varies from one child or one man to another, is it always possible to repair the defect? If this inequality is compensated for in the long run, it can only be through exercise, hard work and expenses that delay progress in the career. One of these steeds will have reached the goal before the other has loosened his inflexible muscles and stiff legs. Between the latter, how many will always keep a heavy, ponderous gait!

Page 27. - Yet he himself (Rousseau) is an example of the power of chance... What particular accident brought him into the career of eloquence? That's his secret; I don't know.

But I do know, and I'm going to tell you. The Académie de Dijon proposed for its prize subject: Si les sciences étaient plus nuisibles qu'utiles à la société. I was at the Château de Vincennes at the time. Rousseau came to see me, and consulted me about the position he would take on the question. "You'll take the side that no one else will take. - You're right," he replied; and he worked accordingly.

I left Rousseau there, came back to Helvétius and told him: "It's no longer me who's in Vincennes, it's the citizen of Geneva. I arrived. The question he asked me, I asked him; he answered me as I answered him. And you think that I would have spent three or four months shoring up a bad paradox with sophisms; that I would have given those sophisms all the color he gave them; and that afterwards I would have made a philosophical system out of what had been at first only a witticism? Credat judæus Apella, non ego.

Rousseau did what he had to do, because he was him. I would have done nothing, or anything else, because I would have been me.

And when Helvétius ends Rousseau's paragraph with the words: "Rousseau, along with an infinite number of illustrious men, can therefore be considered one of the masterpieces of chance... I ask myself if this can have any other meaning than the following: he was a barrel of gunpowder or fulminating gold that might have remained unexploded had it not been for the spark that left Dijon and ignited it?

To claim with the author that it was the spark that made the gunpowder or the fulminant gold would be no more or less absurd than claiming that it was the fulminant gold or the gunpowder that made the spark.

Rousseau is no more a masterpiece of chance than chance was a masterpiece of Rousseau.

If the impertinent question of Dijon had not been proposed, would Rousseau have been less able to make his speech?

Demosthenes was known to be eloquent when he spoke, but he was eloquent before he opened his mouth.

Thousands of centuries ago, the dew of heaven fell on rocks without making them fertile. Sown lands wait for it to produce, but it does not sow them.

How many men have died; and how many more will die without having shown what they were! I would compare them to superb paintings hidden in a dark gallery where the sun will never enter, and where they are destined to perish without ever having been seen or admired.

Let us be circumspect in our contempt; it could easily fall on a man who is better than we are.

What I think of the little coincidences to which Helvétius attributes the formation of a great man, I would willingly think of those other little coincidences to which the destruction of great empires is just as gratuitously attributed.

Empires ripen and rot in the long run like fruit. In this state, the most frivolous event brings about the dissolution of the empire, and the lightest tremor the fall of the fruit; but the fall and dissolution had been prepared by a long series of events. A moment later, and the empire would have dissolved and the fruit would have fallen of its own accord.

Do we need an even more apt comparison? A man is healthy and vigorous in appearance. A small pimple appears on his thigh, accompanied by a slight itch: he rubs it, the pimple is flayed, and the flay, which is not a line in diameter, becomes the center of a gangrene whose rapid progress causes the thigh, the leg and the whole machine to rot. Is it the slight abrasion, the small pimple or the man's continuous intemperance that I will regard as the real cause of his death?

Page 28. - Is it necessary, in defense of his opinion, to maintain that the absolutely brute man, the man without art, without industry and inferior to every known savage, is nevertheless both more virtuous and happier than the polite citizen of London and Amsterdam? Rousseau maintains this.

I think Jean-Jacques' attack on the social state is weak. What is the social state? It's a pact that brings together, unites and binds together a multitude of previously isolated beings. Those who reflect deeply on the nature of the savage state and that of the policed state will soon realize that the former is necessarily a state of innocence and peace, and the latter a state of war and crime; He will soon realize that more wickedness of all kinds is committed, and must be committed, in one day, in one of the three great capitals of Europe than is committed, and can be committed, in a century in all the savage hordes of the world. So the savage state is preferable to the police state. I deny it. It's not enough to have shown me that there are more crimes, you have to show me that there is less happiness.

CHAPTER IX.

Page 55 - The pagan religion has no dogmas.

Is this really true? The gods each had their own story. What name should be given to this history? Anyone who questioned the gallantry of Venus or mocked the love affairs of Jupiter was called impious, persecuted and condemned to death. An eumolpid was no less intolerant than a parish vicar.

Pagan festivals were rare.

You haven't consulted Ovid's Fastes on this. I believe they were more frequent, but perhaps less rigorously observed than ours.

Page 58. - It is easy to change the religious opinions of a people.

I don't think so. In general, we don't know how a prejudice is established, and even less how it ceases among a people. Tomorrow, the king would have one of his brothers hanged for a crime, and the punishment would be no less dishonorable among us; the day after tomorrow, he would have the father of a hanged man sitting at his table, and that father's daughters would not find husbands, even among the courtiers. If it is so difficult to destroy errors that have for them only their generality and their antiquity, how does one overcome those that are as general, as old and more accompanied by terrors, backed by the threat of the gods, sucked with milk and preached by mouths respected and stipendiated for this purpose? I know of only one way to overthrow a cult, and that is to make its ministers contemptible by their vices and their indigence. [It's all very well for philosophers to demonstrate the absurdity of Christianity, but the religion will only be lost when beggars in ragged cassocks offer mass, absolution and the sacraments on the cheap at the gates of Notre-Dame or Saint-Sulpice, and when these rascals can be asked for daughters. That's when a sensible father would threaten to wring his son's neck if he wanted to be a priest. If Christianity is to abolish itself, it is as paganism ceased ; and] paganism only ceased when the priests of Serapis were seen begging alms from passers-by at the entrance to their superb buildings, when they became involved in amorous intrigues, and when the sanctuaries were occupied by old women who had a fateful goose beside them, and who offered to tell young boys and girls their good fortune for a penny or two of our currency. So what was the moment that needed to be hastened? The time when the regulars of Saint-Roch will say to our nephews: "Who wants a mass? Who wants one for a penny, for two pennies, for a liard?" and we'll read above their confessionals as we do at the barber's door: Céans on absout de toutes sortes de crimes à juste prix.

The substitution of the goddess Renommée for the Blessed Virgin is a chimera that will not come true in a thousand years.

The combination of the titles Summus Pontifex and Imperator does not seem to me to be without unfortunate consequences.

It would be a great evil for a doctor to be a priest; it would perhaps be a much greater evil for a priest to be a king.

I hate all the Lord's anointed, whatever their title.

The priest (you say) will always be subordinate to the sovereign.

How do you know this? It's very convenient to be able to use God's name to do evil.

Monsieur Helvétius, it's that God is a bad machine, from which nothing worthwhile can be made; it's that the alloy of lies and truth is always vicious, and that we need neither priests nor gods.

Page 59 - Let the magistrate be clothed with both temporal and spiritual power, and all contradiction between religious and patriotic precepts will disappear.

Yes, if the magistrate is always a good man. But if he is a rascal, as is usually the case, he will be a hundred times more powerful and dangerous.

The author ends chapter XV with this intrepid conclusion: that the apparent inequality between the minds of different men cannot be regarded as proof of their unequal ability to have one.

It seems to me that, all infected with the same prejudices and subjected to the same bad education, if we see inequality between minds, it is to the unequal ability to have it that we must relate it.

Page 60 - Here the author seems tormented by some scruple. Whatever the national education system, it will not be possible (he says) to turn all citizens into people of genius.

That's my belief. As for people of spirit and sense, he promises us as many as we please. This is quite contrary to the nature of man, the nature of society and the experience of all centuries. Philosopher, my friend, among those Greeks and Romans of whom you make such a fuss, men of genius were counted by their fingers, and fools and madmen abounded as much there as among us. It is in the eternal order that the monster called a man of genius is always infinitely rare, and that the man of wit and sense is never common.

What a book Helvétius's would have been, had it been written in Montaigne's time and language! It would be as much above the Essais as the Essais are above all the moralists who have appeared since.

I don't know how Helvetius felt about Montaigne, or how familiar he was with reading him, but there is a great deal of similarity between their ways of seeing and saying. Montaigne is a cynic, and so is Helvétius; they both abhor pedants; the science of morals is for both of them the science par excellence; they give a lot to circumstances and chance; they have imagination, a great deal of familiarity in their style, boldness and singularity in their expression, and metaphors of their own. Helvétius in Montaigne's time would have had more or less the same style, and Montaigne in Helvétius's time would have written more or less like him; that is, he would have had less energy and more correctness, less originality and more method.

NOTES.

Page 63. - You, my friend Naigeon, who so well scorned the endiamanté Russian Czernischew, for preferring the English to the French, I denounce and recommend to you n°9 of this page; above all, do not forget that he who assumes from French philosophers the general spirit of the nation, knows neither their works nor their persons.

Page 64. - Why, despite the choice of subjects and the best use of their talents, has the society of Jesus produced so few great men? Helvétius gives several good reasons; but the main one, which he has omitted, is that they were dwarfed, exhausted, stultified by twelve years of preceptorship: they spent the time needed to spread the wings of genius crawling with children.

Page ibid. - You can make good Savoyards all you want; great generals, great ministers, great magistrates, that's another matter. However stupid one may be, one soon knows how to sweep a chimney; one does not learn just as easily how to purge a society of its luxury, its prejudices, its vices and its bad laws. Helvétius is a jack of all trades.

Page 65. - I don't know whether genius can be detected in childhood; as for character, there is no room for doubt. However, Helvétius indiscriminately attributes the creation of both to education and chance, to the exclusion of nature and organization.

I think that a child drawn towards a science or a year by an irresistible inclination which is detected from infancy, will perhaps only be mediocre; but I have no doubt that applied to anything else, it will not be bad.

Page 66. - How many men of genius we owe to accidents!

Men of genius are, it seems to me, soon numbered, and fruitless accidents are innumerable. Accidents don't produce anything, any more than a pickaxe digging the mines of Golconde produces a diamond.

Whoever you are, man of genius or fool, good man or bad, dig as deep as you can into the history of your life, and you will always find at the origin of the events that have led you either to happiness or misfortune, either to illustration or obscurity, some frivolous circumstance to which you will relate your whole destiny. But if you are a fool, rest assured that, disregarding this fatal circumstance, you would have arrived at contempt by another route. But wicked, be in no doubt that, apart from this incident which you charge with imprecations, you would have fallen into misfortune by some other route. But as a man of genius, you're ignoring yourself if you think that it was chance that made you; all its merit is to have produced you: it drew back the curtain that was hiding nature's masterpiece from you and others. Genius and stupidity, vice and virtue, only need time to get their true chance. The honest man, the clever man, may die too soon; for the fool and the wicked, they always die on time.

Page 67. - Jean-Jacques is so born for sophistry, that the defense of truth fades in his hands; it seems as if his conviction stifles his talent. Propose two means to him: one peremptory, but didactic, sententious and dry; the other precarious, but apt to engage his imagination and yours, to provide interesting and powerful images, violent movements, pathetic tableaux, figurative expressions, to astonish the mind, move the heart, raise the flood of passions; it's to the latter that he'll stop... I know this from experience. He cares much more about being eloquent than truthful, eloquent than demonstrative, brilliant than logical, dazzling you than enlightening you. Whatever praise Helvétius may have for him, he did not believe that a single one of his works would go down to posterity; that's how he explained it to me, but in a low voice; he feared literary quarrels, and he was right.

Page 69. - This praise of passions is true; but how can we fail to realize, in doing so, that we are forging weapons against ourselves? Will education or chance make men born cold passionate? Are not passions the effects of temperament, and is temperament anything other than the result of organization? If there's a spark, your breath can ignite a flame, but the first spark has to be there.

In truth, all this sublime extravagance of Helvétius would have provided an excellent scene for Molière, the counterpart to that of the Pyrrhonian: "Without passion, there are no needs, no desires; without needs and desires, there is no mind, no reason;" Helvétius says it. But let him teach us how education or accidents can create true passion in someone who has been denied it by nature. I'd just as soon make sure that a eunuch was inspired with the fury of women: and how many men nature has castrated! some lack testicles for one thing, others lack them for another. Each must mate with the Muse that suits him, the only one with whom he feels and finds himself; he is useless or has only a false erection with the others: they would be badly caressed.

To hear him tell it, you just have to want it to be it. How true that is!

Page 72. - Women should conceive so much veneration for their beauty and favors, that they believe they should share them only with men already distinguished by their genius, courage and probity.

A platonic idea, a vision contrary to nature. They have to crown an old hero, but they have to sleep with a young man. Glory and pleasure are two very different things.

In this way, their favors would become an encouragement to talent and virtue. - But what about the propagation of the species?

Whenever we invent a means of honoring ourselves, if that means is contrary to nature, it always happens that we have only succeeded in extending the path of dishonor.

Do you want to have many dishonored wives? Honor those who will throw themselves on their husbands' pyres. Haven't you had enough yet? Attach their honor to chastity. Do you want more? Sacrifice their inclination to ambition, fortune and all those vanities foreign to the sexual organ, to which you will never inspire any instinct other than its own. It has its object like the eye, and the legislator who would condemn, on pain of ignominy, the eye to look only at certain important objects, would be insane.

Whatever advantage one might imagine in depriving women of the ownership of their bodies, in order to make them public property, it's a kind of tyranny the idea of which revolts me, a refined way of increasing their servitude, which is already only too great. Let them say to a captain, a magistrate or any other illustrious citizen: "Yes, you are a great man, but you are not my doing. The fatherland owes you honors, but let it not be at my expense. I am free, you say, and by sacrificing my taste and my senses you subject me to the vilest function of the last of the slaves. We have aversions of our own that you neither know nor can know. We are in torment in moments that would hardly have the slightest inconvenience for you. You dispose of your organs as you please; ours, less indulgent, don't always agree with our hearts. Do you want to hold in your arms only a woman you love, or does your happiness require that you be loved? Is it enough for you to be happy, and would you be so insensitive as to neglect the happiness of another? Why, because you have slaughtered the enemies of the State, must we undress in your presence, let your curious eye roam over our charms, and join in with the victims, the bulls, the heifers whose blood will stain the altars of the gods, in thanksgiving for your victory! All you'd have to do is forbid us to be passive like them. If you're a hero, feel like one: refuse a reward that the fatherland has no right to grant you, and don't confuse us with the unfeeling marble that lends itself without complaint to the statuary's chisel. Let the artist be ordered to make your statue, but don't order me to be the mother of your children. Who told you that my choice wasn't made? And why must the day of your triumph be marked by the tears of two unfortunates? The enthusiasm of the fatherland bubbled up in your heart, you covered yourself with your weapons and went to seek out our enemy. Wait until the same enthusiasm prompts me to tear off my own clothes and run to meet your footsteps, but don't make it a law. When you marched into battle, it wasn't the law you obeyed, it was your magnanimous heart; let me obey mine. Won't you tire of ordering us to have virtues, as if we were incapable of having any of our own? Won't you get tired of making us think about our duties, in which we see only too much esteem or too much contempt? Too much contempt, when you use us like a laurel branch that lets itself be plucked and bent without a murmur; too much esteem, if we are the most beautiful crown you could ever aspire to. You will not compel my homage, if you think that there is no homage more flattering than that which is free. But I am silent, and I blush to speak to the defender of my country, as I would speak to my captor."

Who would want a woman who dared to express herself in this way? And because modesty closes her mouth, is it honest to abuse her silence and her person?

SECTION II.

Helvétius continues with the same text, namely: that all men commonly well organized have an equal aptitude for the mind.

CHAPTER I.

Page 82 - When, enlightened by Locke, we know that it is to the organs of the senses that we owe our ideas..... we must commonly conclude that the inequality of minds is the effect of the unequal finesse of their senses.

Say by Aristotle, who was the first to expressly say that there was nothing in the understanding that had not previously been in sensation. Said by Hobbes, who long before Locke had deduced, in his small and sublime Treatise on Human Nature, from Aristotle's principle almost all the consequences that could be drawn from it.

Page 83. - However, if contrary experiences were to prove that the superiority of the mind is not proportionate to the greater or lesser perfection of the five senses, we would be forced to seek the explanation of this phenomenon in another cause.

When I see a witty man become stupid following a violent attack of fever, and, conversely, a fool think and speak, in delirium, like a witty man; when I see another lose his reason and common sense through a fall, through a contusion to the head, all his other organs having remained in a healthy state: can I help concluding that the perfection of intellectual operations depends mainly on the conformation of the brain and cerebellum? And can I doubt the certainty of my conclusion, when I compare the progress of the mind with the development of the organs in the different ages of man?

Page 84. - Locke sees less difference between minds than we think.

But less difference is not no difference, and I shall as soon believe that we can give to the animal called the Sloth, the agility of the ape or the vivacity of the squirrel, as to the heavy and ponderous man the character of the lively man.

I believe, says Locke, that I can assure you that of a hundred men, there are more than ninety who are what they are, good or bad, useful or harmful to society, by the instruction they have received.

Locke says good or bad, not ingenious or stupid.

When goodness and badness have as much to do with organization as ingenuity and stupidity, they should not be confused, nor should inner dispositions and actions. Let me explain.

A man who is naturally wicked has sensed through experience and reflection the disadvantages of wickedness; he remains wicked and does good.

A man who is half-witted has sensed, through experience and reflection, the advantages of wit; he would like to have some, but no matter what he does, he has none: he thinks, acts and speaks like a fool.

A strict father forces his son to do a good deed; this father would be a ferocious beast if, grabbing him by the hair and hitting him, he said: Maroufle, be witty. The police lieutenant wouldn't lock him up for mistreating his child, but for demanding what nature had denied him.

Quintilian speaks of an innate laziness of mind peculiar to certain men; but how would Quintilian recognize this primitive vice of organization and reconcile it with an equal aptitude for instruction?

He says that heavy and unscientific minds are no more in nature than monsters.

How many monsters! Quintilian would have shown much more judgment if he had associated imbeciles with men of genius and regarded both as monsters.

And then there's a thought I can't resist, and which I recommend to every reader as a very delicate and very safe principle of criticism: it's that in the speeches and writings of the most moderate and judicious men, there is always a little exaggeration of profession. Locke and Quintilian deal with education, and they will persuade themselves that all our children are equally susceptible to it; and if they succeed in persuading us who are fathers, the more readers Locke will have, the more disciples Quintilian will have. But what happens? It's that a fool gets a fool out of Quintilian's school; and that with the most assiduous care and all the fine principles of Locke, I have made nothing worthwhile out of my son.

The best pupils are usually those who give the least trouble to the teacher. And it's not uncommon for the least educated children to be the best subjects.

What is the reason for these phenomena? In the unequal aptitude for instruction. And where does this unequal aptitude come from? From ungrateful or indulgent nature, from diversity of organization.

I don't claim that this is always the case; but to destroy Helvétius' paradox, it's enough that it's a frequent occurrence.

I'll go further: I suggest to Helvétius that he question all the teachers in Paris, and if he finds a single one who agrees with him, I bow my head and keep quiet.

But if children can be made to do anything, why didn't Helvétius do with his eldest daughter what Nature did with his youngest? He must have been quite stubborn about his system to have stood firm against a daily and domestic demonstration of its falsity.

CHAPTER II.

Page 88. - The soul is a principle of life to the knowledge and nature of which one does not rise without the wings of theology.

And with these beautiful bat wings, to what do we rise? To nothing; one circulates in darkness. And why spoil a work with such sycophancy? Posterity won't hear you, and your contemporaries' theologians won't like you any better.

Page ibid - M. Robinet... If he is the author of the work De la Nature published under his name, I have heard from some of our philosophers that he did not hear it.

Page 90 - Man owes his ideas and his mind to memory.

And to what does he owe his memory, large or small, ungrateful or faithful, tenacious or fleeting? Has it not been our experience that we have never succeeded in giving a certain degree of it to children who lacked it? Has it not been our experience that nothing is so variable between men? Here, then, is an insurmountable barrier for some in the career of the arts and sciences, and a very great inequality in the natural aptitude of all, either for the acquisition of ideas, or for the formation of the mind.

D'Alembert once read a geometry demonstration and knew it by heart. On the tenth time, I fumble again.

D'Alembert never forgets it. After a few days, barely a trace remains.

All being equal, how can it be that in the same amount of time I've been studying, I've been going down the same path as he has?

If memory is lost or weakened by a blow, a fall, an illness... can't a child be born with this organ vitiated by nature as well as by accident? What will you say of this child? Will you grant him the same aptitude for education?

Aren't we almost all, if we compare ourselves to M. de Guibert or M. de Villoison? Don't these two kinds of prodigies demonstrate that there is an organization specific to memory? And if I haven't received this organization, who will give it to me?

- You don't need it, you may say, to be a great man.

- That may be; but don't make the breadth of your ideas and the strength of your mind depend on it.

CHAPTER V.

Page 102. - To say, as the doctors of the school do, that a mode or manner of being is not a body or has no extent, nothing could be clearer. But to make this mode a being, and even a spiritual being, is, in my opinion, nothing more absurd.

So they don't do it. They don't say that thought is a spiritual being, but they do say that it is a mode incompatible with matter, which is quite different; and from this they conclude the existence of a spiritual being.

I don't claim that their system is any more sensible, but I see a great deal of inconvenience in misrepresenting it. When they read this place, "There," they'll say, "that's how they hear us, and how they refute us."

CHAPTER VI.

Page 103. - To feel is to judge.

This assertion, as stated, does not strike me as rigorously true. The stupid feel, but perhaps they don't judge. The being totally deprived of memory feels, but does not judge; judgment presupposes the comparison of two ideas. The difficulty lies in knowing how this comparison is made, since it presupposes two present ideas. Helvetius would have cut a terrible knot, if he had explained to us quite clearly how we have two ideas present at the same time, or how not having them present at the same time, we nevertheless compare them.

Perhaps I was in a mood when I read this sixth chapter, but here is my observation; good or bad, it will remain. From the author's entire metaphysics, it follows that judgments, or the comparison of objects with one another, presupposes some interest in comparing them; and this interest necessarily emanates from the desire to be happy, a desire that has its source in physical sensibility. This is a conclusion that has been drawn from afar, and is more appropriate to animals in general than to man. To pass abruptly from physical sensibility, i.e. from the fact that I am not a plant, a stone, a metal, to the love of happiness; from the love of happiness to interest; from interest to attention; from attention to the comparison of ideas; I cannot accommodate myself to these generalities: I am man, and I need causes proper to man. The author adds that by going up two notches higher or down one notch lower, he passed from physical sensibility to organization, from organization to existence, and that he would have said: I exist, I exist in this form; I feel, I judge; I want to be happy because I feel: it's in my interest to compare my ideas, since I want to be happy. What use will I derive from a string of consequences that are equally suited to the dog, the weasel, the oyster and the dromedary? If Jean-Jacques denies this syllogism, he's wrong; if he finds it frivolous, he may well be right.

Descartes had said: "I think, therefore I exist."

Helvétius wants us to say, "I feel, therefore I want to feel pleasantly."

I like Hobbes better, who claims that in order to draw a consequence that led to something, it was necessary to say, "I feel, I think, I judge, therefore a portion of organized matter like myself can feel, think and judge."

Indeed, if after this first stride we take a second, we're already a long way off.

Who would believe that, after such a frank and firm step, the last of these philosophers also let himself be won over by terror, and ended his sublime work De la Nature de l'homme with visions so strange, so superstitious, so mad, that we are almost as indignant as we are surprised?

To feel is to think, or one does not think if one has not felt... Are these two propositions so diverse that, the first having been found, one can regard the other as a marvellous discovery?

If, starting from the sole phenomenon of physical sensibility, a general property of matter or the result of organization, he had clearly deduced all the operations of the understanding, he would have done something new, difficult and beautiful.

I will value even more the man who, by experiment or observation, rigorously demonstrates either that physical sensibility belongs as essentially to matter as impenetrability, or who deduces it without replication from organization.

I invite all physicists and chemists to investigate what is animal substance, sensitive and alive.

I can clearly see, in the development of the egg and some other operations of nature, seemingly inert but organized matter passing, through purely physical agents, from the state of inertia to the state of sensitivity and life, but the necessary link in this passage escapes me.

The notions of matter, organization, movement, heat, flesh, sensibility and life must still be quite incomplete.

Let's face it, the organization or coordination of inert parts doesn't lead to sentience at all, and the general sentience of the molecules of matter is only a supposition, which draws all its force from the difficulties it removes, which is not enough in good philosophy. Let's get back to our author.

Is it really true that physical pain and pleasure, perhaps the only principles of animal actions, are also the only principles of human actions?

Undoubtedly, we need to be organized like ourselves and to feel in order to act; but it seems to me that these are the essential and primitive conditions, the sine qua non, but that the immediate and proximate motives of our aversions and desires are something else.

Without alkali and sand, there is no glass; but are these elements the cause of transparency?

Without wasteland and without arms, there is no clearing; but are these the motives of the farmer when he clears?

To take conditions for causes is to expose oneself to puerile paralogisms and insignificant consequences.

If I were to say: You have to be in order to feel, you have to feel in order to be an animal or a man, you have to be an animal or a man in order to be avaricious, ambitious and jealous; therefore jealousy, ambition and avarice have organization, sensibility and existence as their principles... could you help but laugh? Why should I? Because I would take the condition of all animal action in general to be the motive for the action of the individual of a species of animal we call man.

Everything I do, I certainly do to feel pleasantly, or for fear of feeling painfully; but does the word feel have only one meaning?

Is there only physical pleasure in possessing a beautiful woman? Is there only physical pain in losing her, either through death or inconstancy?

Is the distinction between the physical and the moral not as solid as that between the animal that feels and the animal that reasons?

Are not what belongs to the being that feels and what belongs to the being that thinks sometimes united, sometimes separated, in almost all the actions that make up the happiness or unhappiness of our lives, happiness and unhappiness that presuppose physical sensation as a condition, i.e. that you don't have to be a cabbage?

So important was it not to make feeling and judging two perfectly identical operations.

CHAPTER VII.

Here is its title: Physical sensibility is the sole cause of our actions, our thoughts, our passions, our sociability.

Note that he does not say a primitive, essential condition, as impenetrability is to movement, which is incontestable, but the cause, the unique cause, which seems to me almost as obviously false.

Page 108. - It is to feed himself, to clothe himself, it is to adorn his wife or mistress... that this ploughman tires.

But to adorn his wife or his mistress, is it of an animal who feels or of a man who judges? When we embellish it, it's sometimes to arouse physical pleasure in others; to experience it ourselves, when we love, it's superfluous dressing.

Page 109. - What makes us love to the point of playing games? Fear of boredom.

But does boredom belong to animals or to humans? What about the one who plays for recreation? What about those who play because they're good at it?

What makes us love the big game?

Laziness, which, of all the ways to make a great fortune, chooses the most hazardous, but the shortest. Greed, which pounces on someone else's spoils without regard for their despair. Pride, etc. What is animal and physical about these different motives?

Why do we help those who suffer? Because we identify with him.

But whose honest and sublime identification is it? Is it the physical man or the moral man?

Never have so many true things been said and so many false consequences drawn, never has so much wit been shown with so little logic. You'd have to be strangely stubborn in one opinion to assert that anyone who opens his purse to the destitute secretly intends to have a good bed, a good supper and to sleep with his neighbor.

I beg the reader's pardon, but I'm about to say something filthy, dirty, in the worst possible taste, something you'd hear at the market, but more decisive than a thousand lines of reasoning. Well, Monsieur Helvétius, all the plans of a great king, all the labors of a great minister or magistrate, all the meditations of a politician, of a man of genius, are reduced to f..... a blow in the morning and making a turd in the evening. And you call this moralizing and human knowledge?

Do you deny the beautiful clandestine actions? Do you disguise them all in the hope that chance will reveal them? What is the physical purpose of these actions?

What does he who sacrifices his life propose to himself? Were Codrus and Decius going to seek some physical pleasure in a sepulchre, at the bottom of an abyss?

The evil-doer on his way to the place of torment undoubtedly experiences physical pain, but is it the only kind of pain? Can't you distinguish it from the executioner's strokes?

Remorse is nothing more than the anticipation of the physical harm to which the uncovered crime would expose us.

Yes, that may be the villain's remorse, but don't you know another?

There are pains and pleasures of pure opinion that transport or distress us, without any connection, either implicit or explicit, to physical consequences. I would often have preferred an attack of gout to a light mark of contempt.

I have to walk to Rue Sainte-Anne to chat with a certain philosopher I like, or to converse even more gently with a woman in his neighborhood; but am I only going because I have feet? These two actions are undoubtedly reducible in the final analysis to physical sensibility, but as a condition and not as a cause, goal or motive.

Page 112. - Develop the feeling of friendship, and when, by dint of disfiguring it, you have made nothing of it but physical pain or pleasure, don't be surprised if you are regarded as an atrocious man or an absurd reasoner.

Page 113. - You speak to me again of the enjoyment of a beautiful slave or a beautiful painting; and how do you speak to me of this? Of the enjoyment of the slave, like a gourmand devouring a plover; of the beautiful painting like a physicist considering the solar spectrum. But these are very different pleasures.

To caress the slave, to admire the painting, you have to feel, I agree, but it's as you have to exist.

Without love for beautiful slaves and beautiful paintings, this man would have been indifferent to the discovery of treasure. This is false in every sense.

And if it were the hope of enjoying your mistress tomorrow that would make you happy today, would you be happy with physical pleasure? You confuse the pleasure of expectation with that of enjoyment, just as you confuse present pain with the pain of foresight. When you die of hunger, what do you feel? Failure, contraction of the stomach, a particular and cruel sensation of the organs of swallowing: what do these symptoms have in common with the hunger you foresee, with your worries, your turmoil, your despair? There is so little connection between these two pains, and your attention is so fixed on the evil that threatens you, that all bodily sensation is suspended. It's no longer us you see, it's the image of a man in agony, failing and expiring in horrible trances: a frightening image of what you'll be in a day, in two days, in three days. If you saw a man dying of hunger, you wouldn't hesitate to say, this man is dying of hunger. If you saw a man threatened with starvation, you'd never guess. Hunger is a need, and this unsatisfied need becomes a disease. Would you say that disease and the fear of becoming ill are the same thing? Hunger is in the gullet, the oesophagus, the stomach and the whole length of the intestinal canal; the fear of famine, like all other fears, is in the mind.

Nothing happens to me that I don't see in it the hope of a good or the fear of an evil.

- But because this good and evil presuppose physical sensibility, are they physical?

The author sometimes errs because he is too fine, and sometimes because he is not fine enough.

There is a circumscribed happiness that remains within me and does not extend beyond. There is an expansive happiness that spreads, that throws itself on the present, that embraces the future, and that feasts on moral and physical pleasures, on realities and chimeras, piling up money, praise, paintings, statues and kisses in a jumble.

Page 114. - You assume an "impassive man." But an impassive man in your way is a block of marble. You demand that this block of marble should think and not feel; these are two absurdities: a block of marble cannot think, nor can it think without feeling, nor feel without thinking. So what do you mean by impassive?

- Inaccessible to all bodily pain.

- So be it. What do you conclude from this? That he will have neither pleasure nor pain? I deny it. If he enjoys thinking or expanding his knowledge, he will think; if he doesn't enjoy thinking, he will remain stupid.

- But if he remains stupid, it's because he has no interest in exercising the faculty I've reserved for him, so he won't exercise it.

- And you think he won't have the interest of curiosity?

- I do.

- And you believe that one does nothing for oneself alone?

- I do.

- And you believe that there is no such thing as concentrated vanity?

- I do.

- That although this chimerical being is of a different species to me, he will disdain my praise, especially if he knows the full force of my mind and the full extent of my enlightenment?

- Certainly.

- And that when Newton fought against Leibnitz, it was because of a rivalry of bodily pleasures?

- They were after my esteem. I admit it. And consequently to all the advantages it promises.

- To excellent wines?

- Why not?

- To beautiful women?

- Why not?

- My friend, you are extravagant.

Page ibid. - Your comparison of power to a bill of exchange is charming; but this bill of exchange is payable in money for this one, in houris for that one, in reputation or clatter for a third. Tell me, Helvétius, or rather let's ask Thomas, who makes so much of public consideration, that if it were a red-hot iron he wouldn't hesitate to seize it with his teeth, if he refused Homer's or Virgil's laurel, on condition of being reduced all his life to the most shabby garment, to the narrowest necessities, to a small attic under the roof, in a word to the absolute deprivation of all that is meant by the sensual sweets of life, of all the satisfactions attached to ambition, opulence and voluptuousness. If Thomas answers no, I, who am not so fanatical about literary glory, accept the lot and the condition; I accept for this one enjoyment, impassivity to all others. I think; I write the Iliad with fingers of marble; when I pass by, you exclaim: Here he is, the marvelous block who wrote the Iliad... and I'm satisfied.

Allow me another supposition a little more sensible than yours. You're a king, you owe your crown and your life to a hero, your subject. You are grateful, but your benefactor enjoys rest, health, fortune and wisdom: all that your power would lavish on him in the way of physical happiness, he either despises or possesses. Is there nothing left for you to do for this man's happiness?

- Of course not.

- You're mistaken.

- What, then?

- A statue.

- And what's the statue for?

- Alas, to restore to him the enjoyment of all he possesses.

- But is he crazy?

- Not too crazy.

- But didn't he have wisdom?

- And what did it matter whether he had wisdom or not? He lacked nothing that you consider the motive of all our actions, the sole object of our desires; and his childish heart cried out: "The statue, the statue, I want the statue... The ribbon, the ribbon, I want the ribbon.

"But, silly child, you'll lose your health and rest before you get the ribbon.

"I'll try to regain both.

"- That you'll be envied.

"- It's better to be envied than pitied.

"- That you'll be forced to spend beyond your means.

"I'll ruin myself.

" - That, ruined, you'll be deprived of all life's pleasures.

"There are none without the ribbon; the ribbon, I want the ribbon.

"- But here, read this book, and you'll see that we only want the ribbon to acquire what you'll lose.

"This book is very beautiful, I believe without having read it, but it doesn't know what it's saying. The ribbon, the ribbon, I want the ribbon...".

- That's the story of nineteen-twentieths of men; and believing you were writing the story of the human race, you only wrote your own, and because the woman was your ribbon, you assumed it was the ribbon of all the others. Trahit sua quemque voluptas.

Page 115. - Wherever there are no honors that distinguish one citizen from another, wherever literary glory is unknown, it is necessary to supplement this currency with another. A woman could not be the currency of a fine deed among a people of eunuchs. But even this proves the opposite of your thesis.

Page 116. - In order to go sapping, the ecu given to the soldier must be representative of a pint of brandy or the night of a vivandière.

This is not always true. There is a soldier who would refuse a shield representing only a pint of brandy, or the night of a vivandière: witness the one who, at the famous siege of Lille so well defended by Boufflers, exposed himself to being killed like ten others who had preceded him, and who, when offered the hundred louis promised to the one who would inform on the work of the besieger, replied: My captain, take back your hundred louis, it's not done for money. He who sees honor sees nothing beyond it. He who was given Briseïs as a reward for the peril he ran, did not expose himself to it to get Briseïs. Achilles, which of the two do you want, Briseïs without fighting, or victory without Briseïs? He who is Achilles answers: I want to fight, I want to win.

CHAPTER VIII.

Page 118. - Helvétius and others translate Hobbes' word, Malus est robustus puer, the robust child is a wicked child, which is not always true; but what is always true is that the wicked is a robust child; and this is how I translate it.

Page 121. - Do we want to fool people? We exaggerate the strength of feeling and friendship.

No doubt we sometimes have this deaf and secret motive, but do we always have it? Is it the only one we have? Are we not sometimes the dupes of our own hearts? Can't we believe we're better than we are? Is it so rare to see enthusiasts gifted with gigantic imaginations, who speak the truth when they talk about the ghosts in their heads? They speak of them like the fearful of ghosts, they have seen them as they paint them; this is neither lying nor politics, it is error.

CHAPTER X.

Page 127. - Pleasure and pain are and always will be the only principles of human action.

I agree; and this work is full of an infinite number of maxims and observations to which I would also say, I agree, but I would add, I deny the consequence. You admit only bodily pleasures and pains, and I've experienced others. These, you reduce to physical sensibility as a cause; I claim that it is only as a remote, essential and primitive condition. I contradict you, therefore I exist. Very well, then. But I contradict you because I exist. This is no more than: you need a gun to blow your brains out; therefore I blow my brains out because I have a gun.

Page 128. - It is said that there are scholars who, far from the world, condemn themselves to a life of retirement. But how can we be persuaded that in these people, the love of talent was founded on the love of physical pleasures, and especially on the love of women? How can these irreconcilables be reconciled?

They can't be reconciled. You make an insoluble objection to yourself; yet you answer it; well? that's something else. What a waste of wit! Leave aside all those subtleties that a good mind cannot afford, and believe that when Leibnitz locks himself away at the age of twenty, and spends thirty years under his robe, sunk in the depths of geometry or lost in the darkness of metaphysics, he no more thinks of getting a job, sleeping with a woman, filling an old chest with gold, than if he were approaching his last moment. He is a thinking machine, as the stocking loom is a warping machine; he is a being who delights in meditating; he is a wise man or a fool, as you please, who sets infinite store by the praise of his fellow men, who loves the sound of praise as the miser loves the sound of a shield; who also has his touchstone and trebuchet for praise, as the other has his for gold, and who attempts a great discovery to make a great name for himself and eclipse by its brilliance that of his rivals, the sole and final end of his desire.

You, it's Gaussin, he, it's Newton, which he has on his nose.

This is the happiness he envies and enjoys.

- Since he's happy, you say, he likes women.

- I don't know.

- Since he likes women, he uses the only means he has to get them.

- If that's the case, go into his home, present him with the most beautiful women and let him enjoy them, on condition that he gives up the solution to this problem; he won't want to.

- He's ambitious for dignity.

- Offer him the position of prime minister, if he agrees to throw his treatise on pre-established harmony into the fire; he won't do it.

And would you, born voluptuary, have burned the book of the Spirit or the Treatise on Man that I am examining, to enjoy Madame Helvétius, you who would have cruelly compromised her happiness and your own, if you had survived only six months after the publication of your work? I don't believe it.

- He is stingy, he has a burning thirst for gold.

- Force his door, enter his study, pistol in hand, and tell him: Either your purse, or your discovery of the Calculus of Fluxions... and he'll give you the key to his safe with a smile. Do more: display on his table all the seduction of wealth, and offer him an exchange; and he'll turn his back on you in disdain. Whether you have made the discovery he refuses to yield to you, and are generous enough to relinquish the honor of it to him, provided that, with his library burnt down, he resolves to lose his life in dissipation, abundance, pleasures, the enjoyment of all those physical goods he pursues unknowingly and by such a painful and ridiculous route; you will no more determine him than an owl to become a daybird, or an eagle to become a nightbird.

This is because there is a principle that has escaped the author, and this principle is that man's reason is an instrument that corresponds to the whole variety of animal instinct; that the human race gathers together analogues of all kinds of animals; and that it is no more possible to draw a man from his class than an animal from its own, without denaturing both of them, and without going to a great deal of trouble to turn them into two silly beasts. I grant that man combines ideas, just as the fish swims and the bird flies; but each man is driven by his organization, his character, his temperament, his natural aptitude to combine this or that idea rather than that or that. Who knows this better than me? That's why for about thirty years in a row, against my better judgment, I did the Encyclopédie and only two plays. This is the reason why talents are misplaced and the states of society filled with unhappy men or mediocre subjects, and why he who would have been a great artist, is only a poor sorbonnist or a flat jurisconsult. And this is the true story of life, and not all those sophistical suppositions in which I notice much sagacity without any truth; charming details and absurd consequences; and always the portrait of the author proposed as the portrait of the man.

[What do all these assertions by Helvétius mean? That he was born a voluptuary, and that as he moved through the world, he often came up against personalities and rascals.

And from what I've just said, what can we conclude? That we don't always love glory, wealth and honors, as the currency that will pay for sensual pleasures. The author agrees with the old men. And why shouldn't a young man, commonly organized, be born with the dispositions to the foibles, virtues and vices of advanced age?

How many children, to use the proverbial expression, are born from the wood from which old maids are made, that is to say, fit for everything and good for nothing!

Stinginess is the vice of the old, and there are stingy children. I have seen two brothers in early childhood, one giving everything, the other squeezing everything, and both exposed daily without effect to the contradictory reprimand of their parents: the elder remained dissipator, the younger miser.

The Prince of Galitzin has two children, a good, gentle, simple little boy and a cunning, shrewd little girl, who is always trying to achieve her goals by devious means. Their mother feels sorry for them; up to now there has been nothing she hasn't done to give her little girl honesty, without having succeeded. What is the difference between these two children, barely four years old and both equally raised and cared for by their parents? Whether Mimi corrects herself or not, her brother Dimitri will never escape the intrigues of the court like she has. The master's lesson will never equal nature's lesson.

With no need for wealth or sensual pleasures, Helvétius composed and published his first work. The persecutions he endured are well known. In the midst of a violent and long-lasting storm, he exclaimed: "I'd rather die than write another line. I listened to him and said: "One day, I was at my window; I heard a loud noise on the tiles not far from it. A moment later, two cats fell into the street: one lay dead on the piazza; the other, with a bruised belly, crumpled paws and bloody snout, dragged itself to the foot of a staircase, and there it said to itself: 'I want to die if I ever get back up on the tiles. What am I going to look for there? A mouse not worth the tasty morsel I can either receive without peril from my mistress's hand or steal from her cook; a cat that will come looking for me under the shed, if I know how to wait for it or call it there..." I don't know how far he took this philosophy, but while he was engaged in these rather wise reflections, the pain of his fall dissipated, he felt around, he got up, he put two paws on the first step of the stairs, and there was my cat on the same roof from which he had fallen and where he was never to climb again in his life. The animal made to walk on ridges, walks on them."

Without any need for wealth, honors or sensual pleasures, or with the easy means of obtaining them, Helvétius made a second work, and climbed back onto the same ridge from which the second fall would have been far more unfortunate than the first. Te ipsum concute; probe others, that's very well done, but don't ignore yourself. What was your purpose in writing a work that was not to appear until after your death? What is the purpose of so many anonymous authors? Where does man get this fury to attempt an action at the very moment when it becomes perilous? What can you say about so many philosophers, our contemporaries and our friends, who so proudly gloat over priests and kings? They can't name themselves; they can't have glory, interest or pleasure in mind; where's the woman they want to sleep with, the position their ambition promises, the flood of wealth that will flow back over them? I know some, and you know some yourself, who enjoy all these advantages which they disdain, because they do not make them happy, and of which they would be deprived on the slightest indiscretion of their friends, on the slightest suspicion of the magistrate. How can you, without a pitiful misuse of words, resolve to sensual pleasures this generous enthusiasm which exposes them to the loss of their freedom, their fortune, their honor even, and their lives? They are indignant about our prejudices; they groan over errors that are the torment of our lives; from the midst of the darkness in which we are agitated, each other's mutual scourges, we hear their voices calling us to a better fate : This is how they relieve themselves of the need to reflect and meditate, and give in to the inclination they have received from nature cultivated by education, and to the goodness of their hearts weary of seeing and suffering without a murmur the evils with which this poor humanity has been so cruelly and for so long overwhelmed. They will avenge her; yes, they will avenge her; they say so to themselves; and I don't know what the final term of their project is, if this dangerous honor is not it.

I hear you, they flatter themselves that one day they will be named, and that their memory will be eternally honored among men. But what does this heroic vanity have in common with physical sensibility and the kind of abject reward you infer from it?

- They enjoy in advance the sweet melody of this distant concert of voices to come and busy celebrating them, and their hearts leap with joy.

- What happens next?

- Doesn't this heartfelt tremble presuppose physical sensitivity?

- Yes, just as it presupposes a twitching heart; but is the condition without which the thing cannot be the reason for it? Always, always the same sophism.

My friend, your vessel is leaking on all sides, and I could sink it to the bottom by the example of a few men who have incurred ignominy and endured it in silence for a long series of years, sustained only by the hope of one day confounding their unjust fellow citizens, by the execution of projects of public utility that they were meditating on in secret. They could die without vengeance; they reached extreme old age before taking their revenge.

What is the relationship between the senseless heroism of a few religious men and the goods of this world? It's not to sleep with a pretty woman, to get drunk on delicious wines, to plunge into a torrent of sensual voluptuousness; they deprive themselves of these things here below, and they don't hope for them up there: They give what they have, and have convinced themselves that it is more difficult for a rich man to save himself than for a camel to pass through the eye of a needle: they do not aspire to eminent positions; the first principle of their morality is disdain for corrupting and transient honors. This is what needs to be explained. When a general law is established, it must embrace all phenomena, both the actions of wisdom and the deviations of folly.

Despite the faults I find in your work, don't think I despise it. There are a hundred beautiful, very beautiful pages; it teems with fine, true observations, and anything that hurts me I would rectify with the stroke of a pen.

Instead of asserting that education, and education alone, makes men what they are, just say that you don't believe it.

Say that often our labors, our sacrifices, our pains, our pleasures, our vices, our virtues, our passions, our tastes, our love of glory, our desire for public esteem have a purpose relative to sensual pleasures; and no one will contradict you.

Say that diversity of organization, fluids, solids, climate and food have less influence on talent than is commonly thought, and we'll agree with you.

Say that laws, mores and government are the main causes of the diversity of nations, and that if this public institution is not enough to equalize an individual, it levels a great mass of men to a great mass; and we will bow our heads before the experience of centuries which teaches us that Demosthenes, whom Greece will not reproduce, can show himself one day either under the frosts of the icy zone, or under the brazen sky of the torrid zone.

Your logic is not as rigorous as it could be. You generalize your conclusions too much, but you are nonetheless a great moralist, a very subtle observer of human nature, a great thinker, an excellent writer, and even a beautiful genius. Please try to be content with this merit, and your friends with this praise.

The difference between you and Rousseau is that Rousseau's principles are false and his consequences true; whereas your principles are true and your consequences false. Rousseau's disciples, by exaggerating his principles, will only be fools; and yours, by tempering your consequences, will be wise.

You are acting in good faith when you take up your pen; Rousseau only acts in good faith when he leaves it: he is the first dupe of his sophisms.

Rousseau believes natural man to be good; you believe him to be bad.

Rousseau believes that society is fit only to deprave the natural man; and you believe that only good social laws can correct the original vice of nature.

Rousseau imagines that everything is at its best in the forests and at its worst in the cities; you think that everything is bad enough in the cities, but that everything is at its worst in the forests.

Rousseau wrote against theater, and made a comedy; he advocated the savage man, or the man who does not elevate himself, and composed a treatise on education. His philosophy, if he has one, is one of parts and pieces; yours is one. Maybe I'd rather be him than you, but I'd rather have done your works than his.

If I had his eloquence and your sagacity, I'd be better than both of them.

CHAPTER XI.

Here the author, having departed from the paradox that desires and aversions are ultimately reduced to the pursuit of sensible pleasures and the escape from physical pains, returns to the paradox of the inequality of talents.

Page 131. - Extraordinary memoirs make scholars, and meditation makes men of genius.

The second is false. There are men to whom one can say: Meditate, meditate all you want, you'll find nothing. Knock on that door until tomorrow, no one will answer, there's no one there... And the first is a particular result of organization. Apply this one to erudition, that one to meditation, and you'll have a poor thinker and a common scholar: one will invent nothing, the other will lose the natural gift.

Page 133. - Let a Frenchman spend a few years in London or Florence, and he will soon know English and Italian.

This is contrary to experience, whatever the reasons. Of all European nations, the French have the least aptitude for foreign languages.

So nature gives us more memory than the discovery of the greatest truths requires.

I don't know.

There is only one real and remarkable difference between memories, and that is their breadth...

What about tenacity? It seems to me that those who learn easily forget just as easily, and that those who take the trouble to learn retain for a long time.

CHAPTER XII.

Page 134. - There are five senses.

Yes, those are the five witnesses: but the judge or the reporter?

There is one particular organ, the brain, to which the five witnesses report. This organ deserved a special examination.

There are two kinds of stupid: some are stupid because of dazed senses, others with exquisite senses, because of a bad conformation of the brain. This is where I await the author, who has so far mistaken the tool needed for the work for the reason of the workman, and who has exhausted himself saying: you need a saw to saw, and who has not seen that you don't saw because you have a saw.

You have to feel to be an orator, scholar, poet or philosopher, but you're not a philosopher, poet, orator or scholar because you feel. To desire and enjoy pleasures, to foresee and avoid pain, we need physical sensitivity. But to know and avoid pain, to desire and taste pleasure, there is always a motive that resolves itself into something other than physical sensibility, which, as the principle of taste and aversion in general, is not the reason for any particular aversion or taste. Physical sensibility is more or less the same in everyone, and each has its own particular happiness.

Page ibid. - Not everyone has the same ears, yet in a concert, at the movement of certain tunes, all the musicians, all the dancers in an opera and all the soldiers in a battalion start off equally in time.

First of all, this is not true; and if it were true, would they all have the same disposition to the art of music, would they all be equally affected by it, would they all be indiscriminate musicians?

There is no conclusive induction to be drawn from external symptoms: this one feels only faintly and appears transported; that one is penetrated by a deep sensation and appears immobile and cold.

Helvétius has found himself in the same position as the seekers of either the squared circle or the philosopher's stone: he has left the problem unsolvable, only to come across a few precious truths along the way. His book is a fabric of such truths. Men will not be more equal, but human nature will be better known. Education will not give us what nature has denied us; but we will no longer have confidence in this resource. All our desires and affections will not be resolved into sensual voluptuousness; but the depths of the cave will be better illuminated. The work will always be useful and pleasant.

Ibid. - If among the most perfectly organized men there are so few spiritual ones, it is because the spirit is not the result of the finesse of the senses combined with good education: it is because it is something else again that the excellence of both the senses and education does not give.

Page 135. - Women of genius are rare.

- I agree.

- They're ill-bred.

- Very bad... But does their delicate organization, but their subjection to periodic illness, pregnancies and childbirth, allow them that strength and continuity of meditation that you call the creator of genius and to which you attribute every important discovery? They take the first steps more quickly, but they are rather weary and stop more quickly. The less we expect, the easier it is to please. Women and great men make a name for themselves at little cost; they are surrounded only by flatterers.

The small number of women of genius is an exception, not a rule.

Ibid. - This is because we must not examine the senses in relation to the general effect of their concurrence, without including the correlative organ, the head. To separate one term from the other in this comparison is to make a mistake. The same cannot be said of the specific examination of each of them, considered in relation to its object.

All things being equal, he who has an obtuse palate will not be as good a cook as he who has a delicate one.

The myopic person will be less good at observing the stars, less good at painting, less good at statuary, less good at judging a painting than the person with excellent eyesight.

If your child lacks a sense of smell, he'll starve to death in a perfumer's store.

If he doesn't have an exquisite sense of touch, he'll never even turn a small pivot, and Romilly will send him back to you.

What pleasure do you want him to take, what perfection do you want him to achieve in the art of imitating nature through sound, if he has a shrivelled eardrum and a hard or false ear? He'll yawn at the Opera.

His five senses are excellent, but his head is badly organized: the witnesses are faithful, but the judge is corrupt; he will never be anything but a fool.

Page 137. - How, Monsieur Helvétius, the choice of milk is not indifferent in childhood, and that of food is in adulthood!

The difference in latitude has no influence on minds.

I don't believe it does, if only for the reason that every cause has its effect, and that any constant cause, however small, produces a great effect over time. If it succeeds in constituting the national spirit or character, that's a lot, especially in relation to the cultivation of the fine arts, where the difference between good and excellent is not the thickness of a hair.

These general assertions about sky, climate, seasons and food are too vague to be decisive in such a delicate matter.

Do we think it is indifferent to the inhabitants of a region, to their way of eating, dressing, occupying themselves, feeling and thinking, whether it is wet or dry, forested or open, arid and mountainous, flat or marshy, plunged into eighteen-hour nights and buried under snow for eight months?

The merchants of Paris will tell you what kind of wind reigns in Italy.

Those whose fury for natural history leads them to the Islands suddenly lose their enthusiasm and fall into inaction and laziness.

Hot days overwhelm us, and we are unable to work or think.

If climate and food influence bodies, they necessarily influence minds.

Why is it that our young painters, back from Italy, have barely spent a few years in Paris, and are painting gray? There is scarcely a man in any part of the world whose mood is not more or less affected by the nebulous or serene state of the atmosphere.

Does a serene atmosphere produce cheerfulness, and a cloudy atmosphere sadness? This will be more or less apparent in character and in one's works.

Let's not give too much energy to these causes, but let's not reduce their effect to nothing.

Climate influences government, no doubt, but government influences minds in another way; I agree; but under the same government and different climates, it's impossible for minds to be alike.

Mountain plants are dry, nervous and energetic; plain plants are soft, succulent and weak.

Mountain dwellers are dry, muscular and courageous; plain dwellers are fat, cowardly, soft and plump: and men and animals.

Mountain dwellers become asthmatic; plain dwellers perish of dropsy.

How can it be that the locality will exert its empire so powerfully over the whole machine, and that the soul, which is only a portion of it, and the spirit, which is only a quality of the soul, and the productions of the spirit in all kinds, will not be affected!

Where do you find morons? In the land of goiters, where people without goiters are called crane necks; and that's how you judge necks when you drink bad water.

It is very difficult to write good metaphysics and good morals without being an anatomist, a naturalist, a physiologist and a physician.

Page 137. - The most spiritual fathers often produce only foolish children.

I have come up with a rather singular reason for this, which I give for what it is worth: it is that the resemblances of the mind are like those of the body, which have leaps and bounds. The great-great-grandfather of this spiritual man was perhaps a man of genius.

Then I would say to the author: These silly children, born of parents who have spirit, are nevertheless well organized. So don't say that they were born foolish, but maintain strongly and firmly that they would have had as much spirit as their father, if they had received the same education, and that the care taken to bring them up would have been aided by the same chances. You have spoken in this place according to the truth, but not quite according to your system, as will always happen, inadvertently, to those who support paradoxes. To catch them in contradiction, all you have to do is let them say it.

Ibid. - There are men of genius of all sizes and conformations.

Do you think there are many with a sugar-loaf head, a flattened head, a narrow skull, a dull gaze? Don't big, dumb eyes usually deliver what they promise? What about gaping mouths, hanging jaws, etc.?

A witty man sometimes looks like a beast; but it's much rarer for a beast to look like a witty man; and when we're wrong, it's because the beastly man is much more beastly than we thought.

From which I conclude that all these assertions are hazardous, and that to accuse them of error or admit them as truths, we need very fine observations that have never been made, and perhaps never will be. What anatomist has ever compared the inside of a stupid man's head to the inside of a witty man's head? Don't heads also have their physiognomies inside? And wouldn't these physiognomies, if the experienced anatomist knew them, tell him everything that external physiognomies tell him and other people with such certainty that they have protested to me that they have never been mistaken?

With a little more attention, the author would have suspected that in the combination of elements that constitute a man of spirit, he had omitted one, and perhaps the most important, and his suspicion would not have been too ill-founded.

What is that element? - The brain.

A single well-known fact would have altered all his assertions: that rickets, which extends the capacity of the head beyond measure, makes children precocious in intelligence.

Page 138. - But supposing man had an extremely fine sense, what would happen?

I'll tell you: he would be reduced to the animal condition; he would no longer be a being perfecting himself in every way, but a seeing being. Let me explain.

Why is man perfectible, and why isn't the animal?

The animal isn't, because its reason, if it has any, is dominated by a despotic sense that subjugates it. The dog's whole soul is at the tip of his nose, and he's always sniffing around. The eagle's whole soul is in its eye, and it's always looking. The mole's soul is in its ear, and it's always listening.

But not so with man. There is such harmony between his senses that none predominates enough over the others to give law to his understanding; it is his understanding on the contrary, or the organ of his reason that is strongest. He is a judge who is neither corrupted nor subjugated by any of the witnesses; he retains all his authority, and uses it to perfect himself: he combines all kinds of ideas and sensations, because he feels nothing strongly.

Thus a man in whom hearing predominates over the other senses to an extreme degree, would only allow them as much exercise as the propagation of the species and the preservation of the individual would require; at all other times, he would be like the mole whose den resounds with the slightest noise, a being listening, and always listening.

Hence it follows that the man of genius and the beast touch, because in both there is a predominant organ that invincibly draws them to a single kind of occupation, which they perform perfectly.

The same principle, taken a step further, would explain how the young swallow, who has never made a nest, does as well as its mother; how the young fox, who has never munched on a chicken, forces a barnyard as deftly as his father. But this is not the place to expound my philosophy; my task is to examine the philosophy of another.

Ibid. - These always sterile sensations would retain the same relationship to each other.

That may be; but as the senses instruct each other reciprocally, the relationship of the sensations of the exquisite organ would necessarily vary with the others. How many things this man would teach us! how many facts he would give us to verify! how many he himself would verify through experiments, the results of which he could always announce! How many terms he would enrich the language! Consider that the observations of his marvellous eye could never be in real contradiction with the observations of our ordinary eyes. Suppose a man had eyesight fine enough to discern the particles of air, fire and water; in good faith this man would be of no use to us. I'd just as soon assure you that one more sense would have been granted to him at pure loss to himself and to others.

Ibid. - A sensation is just another fact.

A fortuitous sensation is just one more fact; but a sensation produced by an exquisite and prodigious organ is a prodigious multitude of facts; it is the meeting of the telescope and the microscope. Has the microscope enriched physics with just one fact?

A fact adds nothing to the aptitude that men have for the mind.

To speak like that, after having said elsewhere that education, that a chance makes genius! Isn't the observation of this or that fact the happiest of all possible coincidences?

There is such a thing to which science or art owes its birth, and such another to which it owes its progress.

Helvétius says black and white, as needed.

Ibid. - Such a man would achieve results incommunicable to others.

But why? If we can't achieve his results through speech, why can't we achieve them through education and experience? But there's more: what he would perceive would relate to length, width, depth, solidity and other physical qualities, which he could explain very clearly; and such would be the difference between a perfected sense and a new one. "The man with a perfected sense, speaking to us only of known qualities, would always be intelligible; the other, on the contrary, speaking to us of unknown qualities, could never be heard.

We all feel differently, and we all speak alike.

If the truths contained in the works of Locke and Newton are generally enough grasped, what does that prove? That everyone was capable of discovering them? I deny it.

Page 139. - Strictly speaking, one man's sensations are incommunicable to another, because they are diverse. If signs are common, it is because of scarcity.

I suppose that God suddenly gave each individual a language in every way analogous to his sensations. From the idiom of Peter to the idiom of John, there would not be a single synonym, except perhaps for the words exist, be, and a few others which designate qualities so simple that definition is impossible; and then all the mathematical sciences.

Page 140 - If there are centuries when, like those rare birds brought to an empire by the stroke of a hundred, great men suddenly appear, let us not regard this appearance as the effect of a physical cause.

I agree; but let it not be forgotten that what is more or less true when comparing one nation to another, is completely false when comparing the same society and one individual to another. There is no nation under the Pole, under the Equator, from which we cannot produce Homers, Virgils, Demosthenes, Ciceros, great legislators, great captains, great magistrates, great artists; but these men will be rare everywhere, whatever the government. It would be absurd to attribute their formation to chance and education; it would be no less absurd to assume that a Plato or a Montesquieu can be made out of any commonly well-organized being. As for the diversity of climates alone, I would readily believe that spirits, like certain fruits, are good everywhere, but excellent in certain regions.

Ibid. - It is argued that it is to the fire of youth that we owe the beautiful compositions of great men.

No; but what is maintained, and with good reason, is that they cannot be the product of old age. Youth has too much verve and not enough judgment; old age has neither enough verve nor enough judgment; and one or two rare exceptions prove nothing.

Page 141. - The Voltaire of sixty is not the Voltaire of thirty, yet they are equally witty.

If this is so, tell Voltaire to give us something today that we can compare to Brutus or Mahomet: for if the Voltaire of sixty is the Voltaire of thirty, why shouldn't the Voltaire of eighty-two or three be the Voltaire of sixty? Was the

Corneille of Pertharite the Corneille of Les Horaces or Cinna?

Ibid. - I have never seen two men who jumped as high, who ran as fast, who shot as accurately, who played as well at paume, and even less two men who were equally witty, because it was impossible for that to be the case.

- So you could have identified the difference?

- Not always; but I would often have felt it; and when I would neither have assigned it nor felt it, it would have been there; and there would have been someone with a finer tact who would have discerned it.

Ibid. - The lawyer wins or loses the same number of cases; the doctor kills or cures the same number of patients; the genius produces the same number of productions.

The first two comparisons are pitiful, and the last one is either from a man of bad faith, or from a man who doesn't know what genius is, and doesn't have a grain of it. In the first two comparisons, Helvétius confuses talent with practice. One year, a lawyer loses every case he pleads; the next year, he wins them all. As for the man of genius, he is so little master of himself, that he doesn't know what he will do; and this is the reason why academies almost suffocate men of this calibre by subjecting them to a regulated task. But I'll leave this text, which would take me too far.

Page 142. - The perfection of external organization presupposes that of internal organization.

In other words, a handsome man is always witty, and a beautiful woman is always witty. How absurd can one be?

Ibid. - The explanation of the phenomenon of the inequality of spirits must be sought in some as yet unknown cause.

What does this mean? Is there inequality between minds? And does this inequality have a cause?

- Yes, chance and instruction.

- So this cause is not unknown.

CHAPTER XIII.

Page 145. - If the Malays, says M. Poivre, had been closer to China, that empire would soon have been conquered.

I believe this to be true.

And the form of its government changed.

I deny it. It has never been asked why Chinese laws and mores have been maintained in the midst of the invasions of this empire. The reason is that it takes only a handful of men to conquer China, and millions to change it. Sixty thousand men have conquered this land; what has become of them? They have been dispersed among sixty million people, that's a thousand men for every million; but do we believe that a thousand men can change the laws, manners, customs and habits of a million men? The victor conforms to the vanquished, whose mass dominates him: it's a stream of fresh water lost in a sea of salt water, a drop of water falling into a barrel of wine spirit. The duration of the Chinese government is a necessary consequence not of its goodness, but of the excessive population of the region; and as long as this cause persists, the empire will change masters without changing its constitution: the Tartars will become Chinese, but the Chinese will not become Tartars. I only know of the superstition of an intolerant conqueror that could shake the national administration and laws, because this religious fury is capable of the most extraordinary things, such as massacring several million dissidents in one night. A new religion cannot be introduced among any people without a revolution in legislation and morals. Guarantee China of this event, answer me that the children of some emperor will not share this vast country, and fear nothing either for the progress of its population or for the duration of its morals.

Page 148. - Why do amateurs almost never equal their masters? Why does the advantage of organization not make up for the lack of attention?

It's because, among students, the one who tires the most is often the one who makes the least progress, and that all the application of the first cannot make up for the defect in natural disposition.

It's that in everything, study and the longest and most sustained study must be combined with the happiest natural qualities, which amateurs fail to do.

CHAPTER XIV.

Page 148. - Men, in the presence of the same objects, can undoubtedly experience different sensations; but can they, consequently, perceive different relationships between these same objects?

I don't seem to understand the meaning of this question, for the relui it naturally presents does not permit the author's negative answer.

What is wit, finesse, penetration, if not the ease of perceiving in one being, between several beings that the multitude has looked at a hundred times, qualities, relationships that none of them have perceived? What is a fair, new and piquant comparison, what is a bold metaphor, what is an original expression, if not that of some singular relationship between known beings that we bring closer and touch from some side?

Not everyone perceives all the properties of beings. None feel them and perceive them rigorously in the same way. Very few grasp all the points of contact between them. Fewer still are capable of rendering in a strong, precise and interesting way both the qualities of a being they have studied and the relationships they have seen between different beings.

Page 149. - A blow causes pain to two beings in the ratio of 2 to 1; a double blow will produce double pain in both or in the ratio of 4 to 2 or 2 to 1.

How many inaccuracies and random assertions in all this!

Who told you that pleasure and pain are in the constant ratio of impressions?

A movement of joy is aroused in two beings by a story; the continuation of the story doubles the impression in one and the other, and there's John laughing harder and Peter feeling worse. The pleasure has turned into pain, the quantity that was positive has become negative.

The single blow makes them both scream; the double blow sharpens the scream of one and kills the other.

No, sir, no, objects do not strike us in a constant and uniform proportion, and this is what constitutes the difference between robust and delicate beings: one faints and loses his head, while another is barely moved.

Neither pleasure nor pain can be increased at will: extreme pleasure turns into pain: extreme pain leads to transport, delirium, insensibility and death.

Ibid. - The only affections whose influence on minds is perceptible are those dependent on education and prejudice.

I don't think it's possible to say anything more absurd.

Is it education and prejudice alone that make women generally fearful and pusillanimous, or is it the awareness of their weakness, an awareness that is common to all delicate animals, an awareness that makes one flee at the slightest noise, and stops the other proudly at the appearance of danger and the enemy?

All these pages can only impose on a superficial mind, seduced by an ingenious antithesis.

Page 151. - Do I remember only the snows, the icicles, the storms of the north; only the flaming lava of Vesuvius or Etna; with these materials what picture can I compose? That of the mountains defending the entrance to Armide's garden...

The genre of our ideas and paintings therefore depends not on the nature of our mind, which is the same in all men, but on the kind of objects that chance engraves in their memory, and the interest they have in combining them.

And it all depends on this single cause! But between ten thousand men who will have heard the roar of Vesuvius, who will have felt the earth tremble beneath their feet, and who will have fled before the flood of flaming lava escaping from the half-open flanks of the mountain ; Among the ten thousand people touched by the joyous images of spring, barely one will be able to give a sublime description, because the sublime, whether in painting, poetry or eloquence, is not always born of the exact description of phenomena, but from the emotion that the spectator genius will have felt, from the art with which he will communicate to me the quivering of his soul, from the comparisons he will use, from the choice of his expressions, from the harmony with which he will strike my ear, from the ideas and feelings he will know how to awaken in me. There may be quite a few men capable of painting an object as a naturalist or historian, but as a poet, that's something else. In a word, I'd like to know how interest, education and chance give warmth to the cold man, verve to the regulated mind, imagination to the man who has none. The more I dream about it, the more the author's paradox confounds me. If this artist wasn't born drunk, the best instruction will never teach him anything but to counterfeit drunkenness more or less sullenly. Hence so many flat imitators of Pindar and all the original authors. Why have the true originals never made anything but bad copies?

But, Monsieur Helvétius, as someone who uses the word original often enough, could you tell me what it is? If you tell me that it's upbringing or chance circumstances that make an original, will I be able to stop myself laughing?

In my opinion, an original is a bizarre being who derives his singular way of seeing, feeling and expressing himself from his character. If the original man had never been born, one is tempted to believe that what he has done would never have been done, so much do his productions belong to him.

But in this sense, you may say, all men are originals; for what man can do exactly what another does?

You're right, but you'd have spared yourself this objection if you hadn't interrupted me, for I was about to add that his character must have stood in stark contrast to that of other men, so that we recognize almost no resemblance to him that served as a model, either in past times or among his contemporaries. Thus, Collé is an original in his versification and his chansons; Rabelais is an original in his Pantagruel; Patelin, in his Farce; Aristophanes, in his Nuées; Charleval, in his Conversation du père Cannaye et du maréchal d'Hocquincourt; Molière, in almost all his comedies, but more perhaps in the burlesques than in the others; for who says original, does not always say beautiful, it misses of it of much. There is hardly any kind of beauty for which there are no earlier models. If Shakespeare is an original, is it in his sublime places? Not at all; it's in the extraordinary, incomprehensible, inimitable mixture of things of the greatest and the worst taste, but above all in the weirdness of the latter. The sublime in itself, I dare say, is not original; it only becomes so through a kind of singularity that makes it personal to the author: you have to be able to say: This is the sublime of such and such. For example, Let him die is Corneille's sublime; Thou shalt sleep no more is Shakespeare's sublime. No matter how well I wash my hands, I still see blood; this verse is mine, but the sublime is by the English author.

But I've been solving your sophisms long enough; would you be so kind as to take a moment to solve mine?

You knew the Riccoboni; eh! she was your friend. She had been better brought up and possessed more wit, finesse and taste than the whole Italian troupe put together. She had a death grip on her soul when she left the stage. She spent days and nights studying her roles. What I'm telling you now, I got from her. She practiced on her own, took lessons and advice from her friends and the best actors; she never achieved mediocrity. Why is that, please? Because she lacked the natural aptitude for declamation. Would you say she started too late? She was born in the wings and walked on the edges of the stage. That she wasn't warmed up enough? She blushed in front of her lover, her lover blushed at her; she forbade him the show, he was afraid to go. That she wasn't working hard enough? It was impossible to work harder. That she didn't know the principles of her art because she hadn't meditated on them? No one knew it, had studied it in greater depth or spoke of it better than she did. That she lacked outward qualities? She's neither good nor bad, and a hundred other figures have had their ugliness forgiven by their talent; the sound of her voice is pleasant; it wouldn't have been, that with naturalness, truth, warmth and guts, she would have accustomed us to it. But she lacked neither soul nor sensitivity. She undoubtedly shared with all actors the influence of extraneous causes that either develop or stifle talent, with the difference that, as the daughter of a beloved actor, she had that advantage of which the others are deprived. Come on, Helvétius, no more of these subtleties with which neither of us would be satisfied. Try to explain this phenomenon to me clearly. These happy coincidences to which you attach such powerful effects, she was exposed to every day. Above all, don't forget that the spectator who applauded the father would like nothing better than to do the same with the daughter; but there was no way, she was too bad, she said so herself.

Not everyone is suited to everything, not even to being a good actor, if nature is against it.

La Riccoboni was disgraced by nature: they said so in Paris, they would have said as much in London, in Madrid, wherever she would have been as bad. You, who make these kinds of proverbial expressions common to all nations ring out so loudly, do you claim that these and so many others in which the rejection of nature and the vice of organization are used, are empty of meaning?

And me, you're going to see the Riccoboni's counterpart. I was young, I was in love, very much in love. I lived with Provençals who danced from evening to morning, and who from evening to morning gave their hand to the one I loved and kissed her before my eyes; add to that that I was jealous. I decided to learn to dance: I went underground, from the rue de la Harpe to the end of the rue Montmartre, to take lessons; I kept the master for a long time. I left him in spite of not learning anything; I took him back a second time, a third time, and left him with just as much pain and just as little success. What did I lack to be a great dancer? An ear? I had an excellent ear. Lightness? I wasn't heavy, but I needed to be. Interest? I couldn't have been animated by a more violent interest. What I lacked? the softness, flexibility and grace that can't be given away.

But after having done everything in vain to learn how to dance, I learned to shoot weapons very easily, without difficulty and for no other reason than to amuse myself.

CHAPTER XV.

Page 151. - What is the mind in itself? The ability to see the similarities and differences, the conveniences and disconveniences between different objects.

Is this ability natural or acquired?

- It is natural.

- Is it the same in everyone?

- In all men who are commonly well organized.

- And what is its principle?

- Physical sensitivity.

- And sensitivity?

- Like aptitude, whose effects vary only through education, chance and interest.

- And organization, provided it's not monstrously flawed, does nothing?

- It doesn't.

- What difference do you see between man and brute?

- Organization.

- So if you make a Sorbonne doctor's ears longer, cover him with hair and line his nostrils with a large pituitary membrane, instead of fanning a heretic, he'll be chasing a hare, which will be a dog.

- A dog!

- Yes, a dog. And if you shorten the dog's nose...

- I can hear the rest: for sure, he'll be a doctor from the Sorbonne, leaving the hare and the partridge there, and hunting the heretic by voice.

- Are all dogs equally good?

- Certainly not.

- What! There are some for whom neither the piker's instruction, nor punishment, nor chance does anything worthwhile?

- Don't doubt it.

- And you're not aware of all your inconsistencies?

- What inconsistencies?

- To place in organization the difference between the two extremes of the animal chain, man and brute; to use the same cause to explain the diversity from dog to dog, and to reject it when it comes to the varieties of intelligence, sagacity and wit from one man to another.

- Oh, man, man...

- Well, man...

- Whatever difference there may be between the senses of one individual and the senses of another individual, it makes no difference.

- But when it comes to judging one man's aptitude for one thing and another's aptitude for the same thing, is there nothing more to consider than feet and hands, nose, eyes, ears and touch?

- And what else, since these are the only organs of sensation?

- But does the sensation of the eye end in the eye? Is it the eye that assures and denies? Does the sensation of the ear stop in the ear? Is it the ear that assures and denies? If, by supposition, a man were reduced to a living eye or a living ear, would he judge, think, reason like a complete man?

- But this other organ, which you regard as the tribunal of affirmation and negation, we can't hear a thing.

- That it can be healthy or unhealthy, conformed in this way or another without any consequences for intellectual operations, is an assertion against which a thousand experiments clamor and which you will persuade no one.

- But wait, I'm going back. Does this man you've reduced to a living eye have a memory?

- I agree that he does.

- If he does, he'll compare sensations, he'll reason.

- Yes, like a dog reasons, and even less so. I'll say the same for each of the other senses, and Helvetius' man will be reduced to a collection of five very imperfect animals.

- Not so, please. These animals will perfect themselves through the common interest of their preservation, through their society.

- And where is the link in this society? How does the eye make itself heard to the ear, the ear to the nose, the nose to the palate, the palate to the touch? Where is the link?

- In the whole animal.

- But you can cut off a man's feet without dumbing him down. There isn't a limb of his I can't deprive him of, without consequences for his judgment and reason, if you leave out the head. Do you think a man has a mind without a head?

- No, I do not.

- Do you believe that a man with a bad eye can see well?

- No, I do not.

- And why then do you believe that the conformation of his head is indifferent to his reason?

- Because there are men of genius with small foreheads, large foreheads, big heads, small heads, long heads and round heads.

- But tell me, if someone presented you with a book and asked you to decide whether it was good or bad just by looking at the cover, what would you say?

- That it's crazy.

- Very well; and to judge, what would you ask them to do?

- To open it and read at least a few pages. But no matter how many heads I open, I won't read anything.

- The characters of this living book are not yet known to you, perhaps they never will be; but the depositions of the five witnesses are no less recorded, combined, compared, confronted. I could follow this comparison much further, and draw a multitude of consequences from it, but this is enough, and more than enough perhaps, to convince you that you have neglected the examination of an organ without which the condition of the others, more or less perfect, means nothing, the organ from which emanate the astonishing differences between men, in relation to intellectual operations.

Don't talk to me about chances; there are no happy or fruitful ones for narrow minds.

Don't talk to me about interest; apathetic heads can't conceive of lively interest.

Don't talk to me about strong, continuous attention; weak heads are incapable of it.

Don't talk to me about physical sensitivity, a quality that constitutes the animal and not the man.

Don't talk to me either about sensual pleasures as the principle of the actions of the whole species, whereas this is only the motive for the actions of the voluptuous man; and stop taking primitive conditions, essential and remote, for future causes, and spoiling excellent observations with absurd inductions.

And don't think I'm joking; without a common correspondent and judge of all sensations, without a commemorative organ of all that happens to us, the sensitive and living instrument of each sense would perhaps have a momentary awareness of its existence, but there would certainly be no awareness of the whole animal or man.

Page 152 - Not everyone experiences the same sensations, but everyone senses objects in the same proportion.

Well, they will be instruments tuned by thirds, fourths or fifths; although the tuning will be the same, the sounds rendered will be more or less muted, more or less acute. This, it seems to me, is already a fairly large source of organization-dependent variety.

But in addition to the physical sensitivity common to all parts of the animal, there is another quite different sensitivity, common to all animals and peculiar to a particular organ; either this latter sensitivity is originally only the first, but infinitely more exquisite in this place than elsewhere, or it is a particular quality, which I do not decide: it is the sensitivity of the diaphragm, this thin nervous membrane which cuts the inner capacity into two cavities. This is the seat of all our pains and pleasures; its oscillations or contractions are stronger or weaker in one being than in another: it is this that characterizes pusillanimous and strong souls. You would be a great pleasure to the Faculty of Medicine, whose benefactor you would be as well as the entire human race, if you could teach us how to give it tone when it lacks it, and how to take it away when it has too much. It's only age that has some control over it, as well as over the head. It's thanks to its diversity that, at the very moment when I'm overcome with admiration and joy, and my tears are flowing, one says to me: "I don't feel that, I have a hairy heart..."; the other makes a very Burlesque joke. The head makes wise men: the diaphragm makes compassionate and moral men. You've said nothing about these two organs, but nothing at all, and you think you've done the trick. A man with a very motionless diaphragm either seeks out tragic scenes or avoids them, because they can affect him too strongly and leave him with what we call a clenched heart after the show. He who has this inflexible, stiff and obtuse organ neither seeks them out nor avoids them; they do nothing to him. You can make this man either a criminal lieutenant or an executioner, or a butcher, or a surgeon, or a doctor.

How, you hear nothing of the two great springs of the machine, one that constitutes men spiritual or stupid, the other that separates them into two classes, that of tender souls and that of hard hearts, and you write a treatise on man!

I remember asking you how to give activity to a heavy head; now I'm asking you how to inspire sensitivity in a hard heart.

But there's no stopping you; you'll argue that with these two diverse qualities, men are no less commonly well organized, no less well disposed to all sorts of functions.

What! Monsieur Helvétius, will there be no difference between the compositions of one who has received from nature a strong and lively imagination with a very mobile diaphragm, and one who has been deprived of these two qualities?

You who give so much force to the impulse of one sex towards the other, consider that the vigorous but insensitive man will only be drawn by his passion towards the woman like the bull towards the heifer; it is the ferocious beast of Lucretia which, with a deadly arrow through its flanks, rushes towards the hunter and covers him with its blood. He will hardly write elegies or madrigals; he wants to enjoy, he cares little about touching and pleasing. A burning, abundant, acrid fluid irritates the organs of pleasure; he doesn't sigh, this one, he roars; he doesn't turn his tender, languid gazes, his moist eyelids on the object of his passion, his eyes are sparkling and his gaze devours him. Like the stag in autumn, he lowers his horn and makes the timid doe walk before him; in the corner of the dark forest where he has diverted her, he occupies himself with his happiness strongly, without thinking of that of the being he subdues; satisfied, he leaves him and withdraws. Try, if you can, to make me a tender and delicate poet of this animal. He only has one word, or he doesn't have it anymore.

Page 153. - You can be a poet, orator, painter or geometer at will.

How can one excel in genres that presuppose contradictory qualities? What is the function of a surveyor? To combine spaces, disregarding the essential qualities of matter; no images, no colors, great restraint of the head, no emotion of the soul. What is that of the poet, the moralist, the eloquent man? To paint and move.

If one is not a man of genius in two different genres, it is not only for lack of time, but also for lack of aptitude.

Poetry and painting are perhaps the two talents that come closest together; yet it would be hard to name a single man who has been able to create a beautiful poem and a beautiful painting at the same time.

The poet describes, his description embraces the past, the present and the future; a long interval of time, in the painter, has only an instant. So nothing is so ridiculous and incompatible with art as the subject of a painting given in some detail by a writer, even a man of spirit.

There is quite a difference between the roses on Van-Huysum's palette and the roses growing in Ariosto's imagination.

Here are three very different styles: this one is simple, clear, without figure, without movement, without verve, without color: it's that of D'Alembert and the geometer.

This other is broad, majestic, harmonious, abundantly noble, full of sometimes delicate, sometimes sublime images: it's that of the natural historian and Buffon.

The third is vehement, touching, disturbing, agitating, inclining to tenderness or indignation, elevating or calming passions: this is the work of the moralist and Rousseau.

It is no more possible for these authors to change their tone than it is for the birds of the forest to change their flight. Invite them to try this, and they will go from being original to imitative and ridiculous; their song will be borrowed, it will blend in with their natural song, and they will resemble those whistling birds that begin a modulated tune and end with their chirping.

Ibid. - One is not born with this genius or that particular genius.

This is a very new truth, if ever there was one; for it has been thought and said until now that genius was a special gift of nature that trained man to this or that function that was performed poorly or badly without it, Minervâ invited. Alas! the schools are full of children so eager for glory, so studious, so diligent! they may work, torment themselves, sometimes weep at their lack of progress, but they don't advance any further; while others beside them, light-hearted, fickle, distracted, libertine, lazy, excel at playing. I won't forget you, poor Garnier: your parents were destitute, you were shut away in the town churches, you took down the lamp that lit our altars, the holy table served as your desk, you exhausted your eyes and your health all night long; yet I slept soundly, and you never took the place of dignity over me, nor over three or four others. If Helvétius had practiced the unfortunate profession of teaching fifty pupils, he would soon have realized the vanity of his system. There isn't a teacher in any of our colleges whose ingenious ideas didn't make him shrug his shoulders in pity.

Ibid. - The same attention can be paid to everything.

- No, sir, no; you're wrong. There's no one who hasn't felt that repugnance which we rightly call natural, because it's based on a lack of aptitude that we're forced to admit to ourselves by the violence of our efforts and the lack of success, and woe betide you, if it's unknown to you: equally suited to everything, you were really suited to nothing. The long-legged, slender-bodied greyhound is made to follow the hare at a run, but you'll never make him beg; the big-nosed hound, to beat the plains with his nose to the wind or down; the short-haired, bushy hound, to break through the thickness of hedges and brave the tips of brambles; the barbet, to jump into the water; and if you set out to divert their pace, you'll use up a lot of time and belts; you'll shout and make these animals shout a lot, and you'll only get bad dogs. Man is also an animal species, his reason is only a perfectible and perfected instinct; and in the career of science and art there are as many different instincts as there are dogs in a hunting party.

Ibid. - Why so little genius in different genres?

It's a good question, but let's see how he answers it.

- It's that man...

- Monsieur Helvétius, it's that man, drawn entirely to the favorite object of an innate aptitude, sees only that one. If nature had destined him to become a great man in another career, he wouldn't have had the time to follow it. Spend your life swimming, and you'll be a mediocre runner; run until old age, and you'll swim badly. Men who have one genius are rare; how much rarer still those who have received a double genius! This double gift is perhaps a misfortune. It can happen that one is alternately agitated, tossed about by one's two demons; that one begins two great tasks and finishes neither; that one is neither a great poet nor a great geometer, precisely because one had an equal aptitude for geometry and poetry. I heard Euler exclaim: Ah! if M. D'Alembert had only wanted to be an analyst, what an analyst he would have been!... You have to say to these kinds of monsters: Choose. Helvétius's system is that of a very witty man who demonstrates with every line that the tyrannical impulse of genius is foreign to him, and who speaks of it like a color-blind man. Perhaps I'm like that myself. There is, however, one difference between us, and that is that everything he has achieved has been by dint of meditation and hard work: his first work cost him twenty years, his second, some fifteen: both his health and his life. He is an excellent example of what doggedness and love of glory can achieve. He knows a lot about the region he's talking about, but as someone who's been there, I can see that he's never set foot there.

I've observed two phenomena: when you've seen everything in a question, you don't talk about it anymore.

It's that when the genius despairs of going any further, he stops, gets disgusted and wanders off down another road.

The same thing happens to him again, when difficulties that are easy to overcome have led to his disdain.

Ibid. - Why are men of genius less rare under good governments?

It is because the children of rich parents choose a state more freely, and are more at liberty to follow their natural tastes; it is because genius is a germ whose development is hastened by benevolence, and which public misery, the companion of tyranny, stifles or retards; it is because under despotism the man of genius shares perhaps more than any other in the general despondency of souls. To these reasons add those of the author.

Ibid. - One is born a poet, one becomes an orator: Fiunt oratores, nascuntur poetæ.

This maxim is neither entirely true nor entirely false. Poetry presupposes an exaltation of the mind that almost resembles divine inspiration. The poet comes up with profound ideas of which he is unaware both of their origin and their consequences. The fruit of long meditation in the philosopher, he is astonished, exclaiming: "Who is it who has inspired such wisdom in this kind of madman? I see less verve and more judgment in the orator; but I think that, strictly speaking, Demosthenes was born an orator as Homer was born a poet: only the orator's talent is revealed later; one is a poet in the cradle, one is hardly an orator until middle age. The poet has no tutor, and all the circumstances of life teach us the art of oratory.

Ibid. - To reach certain ideas, one must meditate. Is everyone capable of this? Yes, when motivated by a powerful interest.

You feel so well what you can and what you can't, that lock me up in the Bastille and say to me: "Do you see this shoelace? In a year, in two years, in ten years from now, you must stretch out your neck and accept it, or do a beautiful scene by Racine...". I'll reply: "There's no point in waiting so long; let's get it over with, and let them strangle me on the spot."

If my freedom and salvation depend on the production of a beautiful scene à la Corneille, I won't despair.

Ibid. - In any kind of science, it will always be the generality of principles, the breadth of their application and the grandeur of the whole that will constitute philosophical genius.

And any commonly well-organized man can reach that point.

Ibid. - An alchemist or a goblet player were rare men in centuries of ignorance.

Van-Helmont and Glauber were rare men. Cornus is a rare man today.

Page 154. - Are men of different opinions on the same question? This difference is always the effect either of their not understanding each other, or of their not having the same objects present, or of their not putting into the question itself the interest that it should.

This is not all, and there is a source of their disputes that is perhaps more fertile than any of the previous ones.

However well organized two heads may be, it is impossible for the same ideas to be equally evident in both. I don't believe this principle can be contradicted.

It is therefore impossible for the same reasoning to be equally conclusive.

If this reasoning is linked to the chain of ideas of one of the disputants, it will appear demonstrative to him. If it is not linked, or even crosses the chain of ideas of the other; for the sole reason that he would have to admit several errors to himself if this reasoning were true, he will naturally be inclined to believe it to be false.

Page 155. - All men are born with the right spirit.

All men are born without a mind; they have neither a wrong nor a right mind: it is experience of the things of life that disposes them to rightness or wrongness.

He who has never made more than a bad use of his senses will have a false mind.

He who, poorly educated, believes he knows everything, will be false-minded.

He who, carried away by complacency or vivacity, is precipitate in his judgments, will be false-minded.

He who attaches too much or too little importance to a few objects will be false-minded.

He who dares to pronounce on a question that exceeds the capacity of his natural talent, will be wrong-headed.

Nothing is so rare as logic: an infinite number of men lack it, and almost all women have none.

He who is prone to prejudice will be false-minded.

He who is stubborn, whether through self-love, a spirit of singularity or a taste for paradox, will be false-minded.

And he who is over-confident and under-confident in his reason, will be false-minded.

All interests, all prejudices, all passions, all vices, all virtues are capable of distorting the mind.

Hence I conclude that a mind that is right in every way is a being of reason.

We are all born with the right mind! But what is a right mind? It's the one that denies or affirms things as they should be affirmed or denied. And we are all born with this precious gift? and when nature has given it to us, is it in our power to keep it?

However much I want to agree with Helvétius, why can't I? Why do I persist in believing that one of this author's greatest inconsistencies is to have placed the difference between man and brute in the diversity of organization, and to exclude this cause when it comes to explaining the difference between man and man? Why does it seem to him to demonstrate that every man is equally suited to everything, and that his stupid doorman has as much spirit as he does, at least in potential, and why does this assertion seem to me the most palpable of absurdities? Why haven't all his subtlety, all his eloquence, all his reasoning determined me to pronounce with him that our aversions and tastes resolve, in the final analysis, to the desire or fear of sensual and physical pains or pleasures?

A commonly well-organized man is capable of anything.

Believe this, Helvétius, if it suits you; but bear in mind that it's at the risk of splitting your head unnecessarily, as happened to me, on questions you'll never get to the bottom of. I quote myself, because I'm conscious of my efforts and experienced in my obstinacy. I have not been able to find the truth, and I have sought it with more qualities than you require. I'll tell you more: if there are seemingly rather complicated questions that have appeared simple to me on examination, there are seemingly very simple ones that I have judged to be beyond my powers. For example, I am convinced that in a society even as badly ordered as ours, where vice that succeeds is often applauded, and virtue that fails almost always ridiculed, I am convinced, I say, that on balance, one has nothing better to do for one's happiness than to be a good man; this is the work, to my mind, the most important and the most interesting to do, it is the one I would remember with the most satisfaction in my last moments. It's a question I've meditated on a hundred times and with all the restraint of mind I'm capable of; I had, I think, the necessary data; will I admit it to you? I didn't even dare take up the pen to write the first line. I said to myself: If I don't emerge victorious from this attempt, I've become an apologist for wickedness: I'll have betrayed the cause of virtue, I'll have encouraged man to vice. No, I don't feel up to this sublime task; it would be useless to devote my whole life to it.

Do you want a simpler question? Here it is. When a philosopher is called to the court of law, should he or should he not confess his feelings at the risk of his life?

Was Socrates right or wrong to remain in prison? And how many other questions that are more a question of character than logic! Do you dare to blame the courageous, sincere man who would rather perish than recant, than betray his own character and that of his sect? If the role of this character is great, noble and beautiful in tragedy or imitation, why would it be foolish or ridiculous in reality?

What is the best government for a great empire? And by what solid precautions would one succeed in limiting sovereign authority?

Is there a single case in which it is permissible for a subject to lay hands on his king? And if there were, what would it be? In what circumstances can a private individual believe himself to be the interpreter of all wills?

Is eloquence good or bad? Should the happiness of the present generation be sacrificed to the hazards of a revolution for the happiness of the generation to come? Is the savage state preferable to the police state?

These are not children's problems, and do you believe that every human being is born with the ability to solve them? Without any false modesty, I beg you to exclude me. President de Montesquieu would have put all his strength and a good part of his life into it.

Among a large number of men who are better organized and better educated than most, why does the one who lifts the veil of truth from some important corner gain so much fame? Why exhaust yourself in admiration and praise for what everyone else would have been able to do, had interest and chance allowed it? You slander yourself: come on, my dear philosopher, you're not the child of any of these vulgar causes. Hercules smothered snakes in his cradle, and young Cromwel, in his jaquette, in his father's brewery, held in his hand the axe with which he was to bring down Charles I's head. Bring the same circumstances to mind, multiply them with as many as you like, combine them as you please, and perhaps you'll succeed in reproducing the assassin of a king; but that assassin won't be Cromwel.

Everyone is a poet in his own way, eloquent in his own way, brave in his own way, a painter, a sculptor, an engraver, even a geometrician, a mechanic, an astronomer, like himself and not like anyone else. I'm talking about those who excel. Bernoulli solved the problem of the fastest descent curve in a single line. A skilled sculptor is a long way from an excellent sculptor; a great poet is a long way from Homer, Virgil and Racine. Where does this diversity come from? Why has no one ever seen a man of genius do what another man of genius, whom he had before his eyes and who even served as his model, did?

Page 155. - There is no other kind of mind than that which compares fairly.

That may be so; but there is a difference between the ways in which fair minds compare, especially in matters of some extent. Some laboriously work their way to a conclusion through a tortuous labyrinth that exasperates you with fatigue; others, like celestial steeds, get there in a single bound; some combine sagacity with promptness in their choice of means. Some are called originals, because it seems that no one else would have taken the path, or used the means they have devised.

CHAPTER XVI.

Page 156. - If all men agree on the truth of geometrical demonstrations, it is because they are indifferent to the truth or falsity of these demonstrations.

Indifferent! Ask that of the architect, the painter, the perspecteur, the financial clerk, the engineer, the mechanic, the mason, the shipbuilder, the optician, the surveyor, the geographer, the astronomer, almost every class in the Academy of Sciences.

Would you like to see all these artists emerge from a tranquillity founded on the immobility of their principles? Let a man rise up among them who attacks a formula, a customary practice as vicious and faulty, or who proposes a new one, and you will see the warmth of the protectors of the old method and that of the attackers of the new method. Several great geometers have died protesting against the infinitesimal calculus, which they regarded as an ungeometrical method. When did the arguments cease? When it was clearly demonstrated that this calculus had all the rigor of the ordinary calculus.

Here, as in many other places, Helvétius confuses two very different things: the ease of learning and the ease of inventing. It is no doubt given to many men to learn geometry, but not to be geometers; to hear metaphysics, but not to be metaphysicians. If we grant the title of inventor only to those who take science one step further, either by perfecting an instrument or by applying it in some way, and consequently exclude from this category almost all pure and simple problem solvers, we will find that in the mathematical sciences, which are indeed the most accessible to ordinary minds, inventors are not common.

One man sometimes shows more genius in his error than another in the discovery of a truth. I see more genius in Leibnitz's Preestablished Harmony, or in his Optimism, than in all the works of the world's theologians, than in the greatest discoveries in geometry, mechanics or astronomy.

The solution to the problem of squaring the circle, if it is possible and ever comes to pass, will undoubtedly bring greater honour to the geometer, but may not put his efforts on a par with the unsuccessful attempts of Grégoire de Saint-Vincent, or even with Archimedes' approximation.

Was it in stooping to pick up a truth that was at his feet, or in the immense and fruitless circuit he made to meet it where it was not, that such a man showed the extent of his mind?

If, with a kind of justice, usefulness were not the common measure of our esteem and praise, the history of man's errors would perhaps do him as much honor as that of his discoveries.

Independently of usefulness, there is yet another reason for our admiration for inventors: difficulty, well attested by the unsuccessful work of a long succession of great men, above whom the inventor seems to rise by his success. For the good of the human race, it is important that a truth should be promptly discovered; for the inventor's honor, it is important that it should have long eluded the research of his predecessors. The perfection of the integral calculus will do more credit to its inventor than it would have done to Leibnitz or Newton. I say the same of the general method of obtaining the roots of equations of all degrees: it would have been less astonishing at the birth of algebra than it is today.

Page 159. - It must not be said that pecuniary interest is a vile and contemptible motive: 1o because, isolated and alone, it is not; 2o because it is not exclusive of any other; 3o because there are a thousand honest conditions which can only have this one.

Pecuniary interest debases only when it is the sole motive for an action that should be carried out of honor. He who wins a victory only in the hope of plunder is a vile man. The ploughman who cultivates his land to obtain commodities and money is not contemptible, because he cannot elevate his thoughts and ennoble his labours by the consideration of public prosperity. It seems that honor should be the spirit of all bodies, and interest that of the individuals of which they are composed.

CHAPTER XX.

Page 180 - We must follow experience and never precede it.

This is true, but do we experiment at random? Isn't experience often preceded by a supposition, an analogy, a systematic idea that experience will confirm or destroy? I forgive Descartes for having imagined his rules of motion, but what I don't forgive him for is not having ascertained by experiment whether they were or were not, in nature, as he had imagined them. Meditation is so gentle and experience so tiring, that I am not surprised that he who thinks is so rarely he who experiences.

CHAPTER XXII.

Page 192 - Helvetius is asked to explain how the Augustinians, the Cyprians, the Athanasians and so many others who were not fools, embraced the foolishness of Christianity, and why some of them perished in its defense.

It's because Helvetius and I would have become Unitarians in Athens, under Socrates; Christians under Constantine; disciples of Aristotle, two hundred years ago; Malebranchists or Cartesians, a hundred years ago; Newtonians, thirty years ago. If, in the course of our early years, society is divided into two factions, eager for illustration, we throw ourselves into one or the other, according to our taste, our turn of mind, our character and our connections. The melancholic became a disciple of Jansenius, the voluptuous enlisted under Molina. The quarrels lasted, they persecuted and exterminated each other for nonsense. Disgust and weariness set in; the truth shows itself to a few sensible men: the discussion of a single error leads to principles that attack a hundred others. And what does it matter where talent comes from? Whether the germ of it is in the organization, or whether it is acquired from scratch, it is nonetheless led astray by circumstances. One spends one's life delving into nonsense; time and necessity give it importance, and one never comes back. If I had written Augustine's twelve folio volumes on grace, I'd make the happiness of the universe depend on this system; if I were forced to go and sing matins every night, I'd imagine, I think, that it was my nightly singing that extinguished the lightning in the hands of the Eternal, ready to strike the sleeping sinner. This is how, through the importance we attach to frivolous duties, we escape boredom.

Christ, or Paul his disciple, said that the Church needed heresies; I don't know if he felt the full force of his idea. These heresies are like empty barrels thrown to the whale: while the terrible monster amuses itself with these barrels, the vessel escapes danger. But the fatal moment must arrive, when the dispute ceases: then weapons sharpened on the branches are turned against the trunk, unless a new heresy succeeds the first: a new barrel that amuses the whale.

CHAPTER XXIII

Page 193. - The most sublime truths, once simplified and reduced to the smallest terms, are reduced to facts, and from then on present to the mind only this proposition: white is white, black is black.

But is this reduction always possible? Every problem is solved by analysis or synthesis. Synthesis descends from first principles to a conclusion far removed from them, and analysis ascends from this remote conclusion to first principles. It's true that in both methods, each step is identical to the one that precedes or follows it, but is this identity always easy to grasp? Is it equally obvious to all minds? Is the sequence of steps not often very long, and is every mind in a position to follow it and have it present? Conviction is not the certainty and memory of all these identities, and that in the demonstrative order; for demonstration does not result from each of them alone, nor even from their sum, but from their concatenation. Fermat, I believe, who was not a narrow-minded man, said of Archimedes' demonstration of the relationship between the cylinder and the sphere: Memini me vim illius demonstrationis nunquam percepisse totam; I remember never having felt the full force of this demonstration. There is no geometer, however great, who will not admit to you that he has sometimes lost himself in the length of his demonstrations.

But was anyone who could hear the solution to the problem of the precession of the equinoxes in a position to find it? No. This reduction of a remote truth to a simple fact is not the work of every mind. There is no bad edict from the sovereign that cannot be reduced to this conclusion: So, sire, your good pleasure is that we bridle our harvests; but are there many men capable, I don't say of making, but of hearing this proposition?

It's not just in geometry, it's in every art and science that truths are identical. The science of the entire universe is reduced to a fact in divine understanding. Why, then, is the solution to these problems scarcely on the level of the vastest heads? It's because of this very identity, which makes it impossible to move a stone without creating an infinite number of backlashes, the effects of which must be calculated separately and together; it's because opinions, prejudices and customs must be taken into account. Three excellent minds have agitated the question of freedom of grain trade; a thousand others have read and pondered their works with an interest proportionate to a question where the subsistence and life of an entire people are at stake. Where does it stand? At the first step; and M. Turgot claims that the good or bad of his edict will not be evident for another ten years.

Page 195. - Once genius has seen and clearly demonstrated a truth, ordinary minds immediately grasp it.

This is not true. For a long time there were only three men in Europe who heard Descartes' little geometry.

What could be more identical than the truths of the science of combinations and probabilities? Try to solve some of these problems; try to hear Moivre's De la

Doctrine des chances.

Read Bernoulli, and he will tell you that the art of probability presents questions that are no more or less difficult than squaring a circle.

If these questions can be solved, and if they can be solved by men who are commonly organized, why weren't they solved by the first geniuses?

- Chance is to blame.

- In a nutshell, it's the fault of chance.

There is no time when high truths become commonplace, and Newton's principles of mathematics and natural philosophy will never be commonplace reading.

Page 196. - Newton's system is taught everywhere.

That is to say, the conclusions of his system are set out without demonstration, but the demonstrations have remained and will always remain closed letters for the generality of men.

Ask D'Alembert, and he'll tell you there's such a profound corollary that he's not quite sure he understands it.

The whole of chapter XXIII is a tissue of paralogisms whose images and style do not prevent disgust.

Ibid. - The discovery of the square of the hypotenuse, cited as an example, is the work of an ignorant mathematician. There has never been a demonstration so simple, even at the moment of invention.

- The only privilege of genius is to have paved the way.

- And where does this privilege come from?

- By chance...

That too is too pleasant.

There are therefore truths reserved for certain special men... Whether you speak of their discovery, or of their difficulty, I have no doubt.

Page 197. - Now, to conceive their ideas is to have the same aptitude of mind.

What an assertion! To invent a thing or to hear it, and to hear it with a master, is the same thing!

I once knew a man who had not read four fables by La Fontaine, or two or three scenes by Racine or Corneille, that he thought he had done them; he was so close to the ideas of these authors, that it was only a reminiscence for him. Some found his folly amusing, others were indignant at such outrageous vanity. This was Helvétius' man, who saw nothing above his own little talent.

CHAPTER XXIV.

Page 19S - Chance is the master of all inventors.

The master? Say the valet, for it is he who serves them. You will see that it was chance that led Newton from the fall of a pear to the movement of the moon, and from the movement of the moon to the system of the universe; you will see that chance would have led another to the same discovery. Newton didn't think so; when asked how he got there, he replied: "By dint of meditation... And you will see that the meditation of another would have had the same result; and when it would have produced the same result, you will see that any man would have been capable of meditating just as deeply.

Ibid. - It takes more attention to follow the demonstration of a truth already known than to discover a new one.

It may be true, it may be false. Commonly, a good schoolboy hears in two or three hours of reflection what cost the inventor two or three months of useless attempts.

But if this were always the case, what would follow? That the spirit of invention is as great in the author as it is in the reader. Does he seriously believe that it is as easy to follow a page in his book as it is to write a similar one? He who used to spend one, two, three mornings breaking down a word and arriving at a result of four lines, all the clearer for having spent more time and sagacity clarifying them.

Page 199. - What a miserable comparison between the little wiles of a young girl, and the meditations of an Archimedes and a Galileo! You can pay yourself that kind of money, but others won't be satisfied with it.

Besides, Monsieur Helvétius, don't imagine that I agree with everything I don't contradict.

NOTES.

Page 200 - They are not melancholic, because they meditate.

But they are more inclined than others to meditate, because they are melancholic.

Melancholy is a habit of temperament that one is born with and that study does not give. If study gave it, all studious men would be attacked by it, which is not true.

Ibid. - Glory is the need of some.

If glory is their need, then it is no longer women, a good bed, a good table, wealth, honors or any of the sensual pleasures.

Sad or cheerful, one is studious, but cheerfulness dissipates and distracts. Rabelais forgets his library between two bottles. Next to a pretty woman, Fontenelle's watch no longer marks the time. The melancholic, on the other hand, shuns society, is at ease only with himself, loves retirement and silence, which almost means thinking and meditating incessantly.

After meditation, the cheerful man regains his cheerfulness, and the melancholic remains melancholic.

Ibid. - It's neither the slender woman nor the bent woman that a man usually prefers; if he's young and in a hurry, it's the easy woman. If the fury of pleasure no longer drives him, the je ne sais quoi that enchains him, unbeknownst to him, is the image of some virtue whose model he has in his imagination, and which he finds imprinted on the forehead of the woman he loves.

Page 205. - I would neither assure nor deny that the savage man has or has not any idea of justice, and that he could slaughter his fellow man with as little repugnance as he pierces a deer or a bull with his arrow.

I would be inclined to believe that the savage who takes from the savage the supply of fruit he has made, flees, and that by his flight he accuses himself of injustice, while the robbed, by his anger and his pursuit, makes the same reproach.

Laws do not give us notions of justice; it seems to me that they presuppose them.

Incidentally, this is one of those questions I'd like to have thought about longer before pronouncing.

When you defined man, you said he was an animal that combines ideas. What ideas does he combine, if not those of his rest, happiness and security, ideas that are very close to the notion of justice? Utilitas justi prope mater et æqui.

If a single man were stronger than all the men around him, perhaps he would grow old with no clear ideas other than those of strength and weakness; but he soon learns about resentment, since he experiences it, and knows that the arrow that strikes him from behind will pierce his chest, lay him dead on the spot, and that this arrow can leave the hand of a child. What will he conclude? That it's dangerous to insult a child.

The strong man is not a bronze man. If he were of bronze, he would no longer be of the same species as the man of flesh; and I confess that there would no longer be any common morality between them; for morality is founded on the identity of organization, the source of the same needs, the same pains, the same pleasures, the same aversions, the same desires, the same passions.

Polyphemus was not like Ulysses; he only had one eye, which Ulysses gouged out.

In almost all the author's reasonings, the premises are true and the consequences false, but the premises are full of finesse and sagacity.

It is difficult to find his reasoning satisfactory, but it is easy to rectify his inductions and substitute the legitimate conclusion for the erroneous one, which commonly sins only from too much generality. It's just a matter of narrowing it down.

He says: Education is everything. Say: Education does a lot.

He says: Organization does nothing. Say: Organization does less than we think.

He says: Our pains and pleasures always resolve themselves into sensual pains and pleasures. Say: Quite often.

He says: Anyone who hears a truth could have discovered it. Say: A few.

He says: There is no truth that cannot be brought within everyone's reach. Say: There are few.

He says: Interest makes up perfectly for lack of organization. Say: More or less, depending on the defect.

He says: Chance makes men of genius. Say: He places them in fortunate circumstances.

He says: There's nothing that can't be overcome with restraint of mind and hard work. Say: Many things can be overcome.

He says: Instruction is the only source of difference between minds. Say: That's one of the main ones.

He says: Nothing is made of one man that cannot be made of another. Say: It sometimes seems that way to me.

He says: Climate has no influence on minds. Say: We give it too much credit.

He says: Legislation and government alone make a people stupid or enlightened. Say: I grant it of the mass; but there was a Sâadi, great physicians, under the caliphs.

He says: Character depends entirely on circumstances. Say: I think they modify it.

He says: Man is given the temperament he wants; and whatever temperament he has received from nature, he has neither more nor less aptitude for genius. Say: Temperament is not always an invincible obstacle to the progress of the mind.

He says: Women are susceptible to the same education as men. Say: We could raise them better than we do.

He says: Everything that emanates from man resolves, in the final analysis, into physical sensibility. Say: As a condition, but not as a motive.

He says: It often costs more to hear a demonstration than to find a truth. Say: But that doesn't prove the equality of genius.

He says: All men are equally suited to everything. Say: To many things.

He says: The so-called ladder that separates minds is a chimera. Say: Perhaps it's not as long as we imagine.

And so, of all his assertions, none is either absolutely true or absolutely false.

One would have had to be very stubborn or very clumsy not to have noticed this, and not to have erased the light stains on which the envy of some, the hatred of others, will lean without measure, and which will relegate a work full of experience, observations and facts, to the class of systematic, so justly decried by the author.

For any impartial and sensible reader, Helvétius' book will be excellent, with all its faults. It will arouse great cries, because many powerful men are attacked in it, because rare men are relegated to the common class from which they have only been drawn by circumstances unflattering to their vanity; but these cries will not last long, because the author is dead and we must forego the sweet satisfaction of losing him, which would infallibly have happened, had the work been published during his lifetime.

I judged it too harshly on the basis of the manuscript: it seemed to me to be no more than a rather insipid paraphrase of a few bad lines from the Book of the Spirit; I relegated it to the class of those mediocre works whose boldness was all their merit, and which only came out of obscurity by the sentence of the magistrate who condemned them to the fire. I've changed my mind; I value and highly value this treatise De l'Homme; I recognize in it all the merits of a good writer and all the virtues that characterize an honest man and a good citizen. I recommend its reading to my compatriots, but above all to the heads of state, so that they may know once and for all the influence of good legislation on the lustre and happiness of the empire, and the necessity of a better public education; so that they may rid themselves of a prejudice which only shows their ineptitude, that the scholar, the philosopher, is only a factious subject and would only be a bad minister. I recommend it to parents, so that they do not despair too easily of their children; to men vain of their talents, so that they know that the distance which separates them from the common of their fellow men is not as great as their pride persuades them; to all authors, so that they are astonished at the strange absurdity to which a mind of a temperament which was not ordinary, but too strongly occupied with its opinion, can be led, and so that they become more circumspect.

There are places where Helvétius falters, others where the contradiction is so palpable, the objection so strong, the answer so weak, that it is difficult for the author not to have had some suspicion of his error. Was he held back by the shame of retracting his statement? Did he want to create a sensation and publish a work that would be contradicted and illustrated by even sensible criticism? Did he prefer to have his own separate corner among the philosophers and by singular opinions, than to be confused in the crowd with more common truths and less piquant ideas?

He himself is an example of a phenomenon he has noticed: how excellent minds have fallen and remained in palpable error. It was enough for them to have defended them for a long time. You don't convert a man who has written folios on a piece of nonsense; that man would be a hero of his kind, if he had the courage to condemn his life's work to the fire.

A professor of theology found a very subtle answer to I don't know what difficulty was proposed to him against the truth of religion; and there he was, who, from being an unbeliever, became a believer, precisely as if this objection, even solidly resolved, no longer remained to be solved; but his vanity was interested in regarding it as the most important, and this is what he did. At every step, we find the scene of the dancing master and the master-at-arms, where we laugh at ourselves every day.

He says: The correctness of the mind depends on the comparison of ideas and the care with which one observes. Say: Not every mind is fit to compare all ideas; not every mind is capable of attention.

He says: Always pursue happiness, never attain it; on pain of falling back into boredom, experiencing it far below your expectation. Say: If nature, work or opportunity offers me the means to be happy, I'll seize it, I'll seize it quickly, I won't be afraid of running out of desires. I won't give my imagination time to conjure up an enjoyment I'd find less sweet; I'll stretch out my arms to the pleasure that's coming, but I don't want to hold them out too long; it's a tiring position to be in. I'll chase after the pleasure that's slipping away, but I won't go overboard, I'll arrive with weariness and disgust. A miser's or a coquette's illusions, silly illusions, flat deceit; so the coquette grows old with pain and regret, the miser dies in despair.

He says: Love emboldens the weakest animal. Say: Yes, the animal; but man, the tender and delicate man, he stammers, he trembles, he gets confused, he doesn't know what he's saying or what he's doing.

He says: It is on the stem of physical pain and pleasure that all our sorrows and pleasures gather, and I reveal a great truth. Tell him: But this great truth is not general. Saint-Mard was asked where he got all the evil he thought of man. In me, he replied; and his answer had only one flaw, which was to believe that everyone was like him.

He said: Great memory is exclusive of a great mind. Add: But memory is a quality of organization; a man organized in this way therefore does not have the same natural aptitude for wit and genius as another man, and the source of their difference will be in organization; it will be the case of the man with a great memory and the man with an honest memory as of the downward dog and the greyhound: the soul of the one is carried entirely to its nose, and the soul of the other entirely to its eyes. And this is the origin of the variety of minds in the human species, and of the variety of instincts between animals. Each being naturally does what it can do best, with the most pleasure and the least pain. Add: You have forgotten, Monsieur Helvétius, that no organization is exclusive of any talent.

He says: The man of good society obtains little esteem, because he does not make himself useful to men. Say: And he saves them from boredom. A good storyteller is a very essential man where people are very bored; he is highly esteemed, desired and sought after. This was Abbé Makarty's role in Constantinople, where he became a storyteller like a barber. He had a lot of practice, and you shouldn't be surprised, if you remember what you said about boredom.

He said: What good is a great memory? Say: To exclude genius. It's not me, it's you who claim it; hence it happens that you rightly answer the objection that isn't made to you, and raise one that you'll never answer. It's that the man with a great memory has too much of the same brown color on his palette, too much inclination to use it, and paints black or gray.

He says: Let's not complain about too little memory. Say: But if I complain of too much, which removes me from the class of talented men, you'll allow me.

He says: Sapho, Hypathie and Catherine were women of genius. Add: And from this small number I conclude that there is an equal aptitude for genius in both sexes, and that a swallow makes a spring. He says: Men have been great in every corner of the earth where they have experienced no foreign influence that has dwarfed them. Say: Equally tall, I don't believe.

He says: The nature of the mind consists in observing relationships. Add: But is it the ear that observes and compares relationships? No. Does the eye observe and compare relationships? No. They receive impressions, but the comparison is made elsewhere. This operation doesn't belong to any of the senses, so who does it belong to? The brain, I think. What's the point of putting the senses on trial, if you don't demonstrate that anything can be done with a commonly well-organized brain? What, a vessel in the head a little more or less dilated, one of its bones a little more or a little less sunken, the slightest embarrassment of circulation in the cerebellum, a fluid a little too much or not fluid enough, a little prick in the pie-mother makes a man stupid; and the total conformation of the bony box and the soft cheese it contains and the nerves implanted in it will do nothing to the operations of the mind! I'm afraid you've overlooked the two main springs of the machine, the brain and the diaphragm.

He says: What do I care about diversity of organization? It's enough for me that it pre-exists, even at birth. Say: Yes, that's enough for you to be wrong and your conclusion false. These causes are born different and are nonetheless equally capable of the same effects.

He says: The use of bad water, coarse food, disordered appetites do nothing to the mind. Add: Even though they stultify man in the long run? Nor climate, though it is a cause whose effect does not cease? Nor the locality, though the man of the mountain is lively and nervous, and the man of the plain heavy and full. Say: If the freshness of the organs does not produce beautiful works, their caducity does produce bad ones. But aren't there old children and young old men? What reasonable equality will you establish between them? How will you make this immense dawn, which the enormous volume of the accelerated waters of the torrent barely moves, move by the trickle of this stream?

He says: The Voltaire of thirty and the Voltaire of sixty are equally witty. Say: Where did you get that? The Voltaire of sixty is the parrot of the Voltaire of thirty, and that's what imposes itself on you. The old man is no longer getting rich, he's living off his property, his harvest is done, his granaries are full. His field can now become barren, without his expenses being cut back.

He says: One cannot have been oneself and another. Add: We must therefore rely a little on what another tells us about him.

He says: Why doesn't the happy disposition of nature counterbalance in the amateur the small degree of extra attention that the master gives to his art? Say ironically: The small degree of attention? But art is the amusement of the amateur, and the daily fatigue of the artist's whole life; and you call that a little extra attention?

He says: The enjoyment of a beautiful woman may bring more intoxication to my neighbor's soul than to mine; but this enjoyment is for me as it is for him the keenest of pleasures. Say (and God forbid that it should be from your experience) that there are pleasures that pique your neighbor infinitely more than the enjoyment of a beautiful woman. Say that what he may say of himself, he must not say of his neighbor, who is a miser who would not draw twenty louis from his safe to sleep with the beautiful Mme Helvétius.

Everyone has his own kind of interest, and its violence is no less variable in each individual than its nature. There are those who prefer rest to all the pleasures that can only be obtained through care. What can we expect from someone who has put his happiness in laziness? Do you deny the existence of the truly lazy? We all are at times, and some men are born weary.

He says it's astonishing that men should seriously occupy themselves with futile tricks and arts. Say that it's not surprising that a few occupy themselves with what amuses a large number of others. In Roman times, people left Terence's plays for jumpers, tightrope walkers and other such entertainers. The poet who complained about this was right; the philosopher who was surprised by it would have known little about the people.

He says he wants to destroy the marvellous, not the merits of the mind. Say that one does not destroy the marvel of a useful, great and rare thing by any cause whatsoever.

If Helvétius had had as much accuracy as wit and sagacity, how many fine and true things he would not have said! It's a good thing he was wrong. There is always something to learn from the works of paradoxical men like him and Rousseau; and I prefer their unreason that makes me think, to common truths that do not interest me. If they don't change my mind, they almost always temper the temerity of my assertions.

He says: The word right mind includes in its extended meaning all the different kinds of mind. You add: Are there different kinds of spirit? You can neither deny it without contradicting experience, nor grant it without abandoning your principles. There are lively minds and heavy minds, but either these different instruments are capable or incapable of the same works. Quidquid dixeris, argumentabor.

He says: The Jansenists said that the Jesuits had introduced pleasure into a ballet, and that to make it more piquant they had put it in breeches; we must do justice to the Jesuits, this accusation is false. You say: We must do justice to the Jesuits, this accusation is true, and I can prove it: Jesuits are men and have no dealings with women. This reason is demonstrative in Helvétius's principles.

He says: Once words are well defined, a question is resolved almost as soon as it is proposed. Say: The words are well defined between this author and me, and it is for this very reason that we disagree.

- But then the question is one of experience and fact, and when you get to that point, you're converted.

- Not at all; the quarrel has only changed its object, and the difficulty is increasing to such an extent that some sensible men have claimed that the facts prove nothing, so difficult was it to ascertain them and apply them precisely to the question.

He says: "A work in which the true meaning of words is fixed can only be executed by a free people. I had the thought, and it was not so much courage as talent that I lacked. Say: This well-made dictionary would put an end to many disputes, but not all. The geometers have some among themselves, they've been going on for a long time, and I don't know when they'll end.

He says: Nothing should be advanced without the support of experience. Say: That is right; but contemplation being sedentary and experience restless, that is, one must be either Aristotle, or Newton, or Galileo, which any commonly well-organized man can be.

I don't know how the author, who knows so many good words, didn't remember this one: it has been said that a happy epigram is good fortune, but that almost never happens to anyone but a man of wit.

How many inventors, and what a poor glory to be one, if the merit was due only to chance, interest, desire or instruction!

He says: The most honest people are not those who recognize the most virtue in man. Tell the author frankly: I don't agree with you. Say that there are difficult actions of which it would be wrong to believe oneself capable before having done them. Say that Codrus, questioned long before his astonishing sacrifice, would have thought of himself as you think of yourself.

We can promise ourselves a courage we never find, a virtue that abandons us in the moment.

We can believe ourselves incapable of a crime we commit, and capable of a great deed we don't do.

The man intoxicated by the expectation of eternal happiness ignores himself and bends the knee before the idols he braved in his heart, but far from the rack.

Let us think neither too well nor too ill of ourselves, without being authorized to do so by repeated trials; let us wait until the last moment to pronounce on our fate and our virtue.

Mme Makaley said that never the sight of a despot or a prince had soiled the purity of her gaze. Mme Makaley had seen her king.

He says that countless experiments prove that men everywhere are essentially the same. Say that if he speaks of one society of policed and free men compared with another society of policed and free men, this is hardly true; that if he means that everywhere a man is a man and not a horse, this is a platitude; and that if he means that in any society one man is essentially worth another, this is an error. Since the definition of a man and a man of spirit are not the same, and since every definition contains two ideas, one of which is the next kind and the other the specific or essential difference, a man of spirit is essentially different from a man, and as essentially different as a man is from a beast.

Good or bad organization constitutes a difference between men that perhaps nothing can repair. Anatomists, physicians and physiologists will demonstrate this by an infinite number of phenomena: open their works, and you will see that this spring, whatever it may be, of all our intellectual operations suffers in an almost miraculous way from the slightest alteration that occurs in the rest of the machine; you will see a slight attack of fever either give spirit or make stupid. Have you never had a headache? You haven't said a word about madmen; yet madness is a phenomenon which, properly considered, would have led you to results other than your own. We see, we hear, we smell, we taste, we touch as finely at Petites-Maisons as in your office in the rue Sainte-Anne, but we reason very differently. Why don't you ask yourself why? If you had asked yourself this question, it would have added more than one essential chapter to your work; perhaps it would have led you to the true cause of the difference in minds, and engaged you in the search for the means, if any, to repair the defect of a principal organ, of this mirror of feeling, thinking, judging, dull, obscured, broken, to the decision of which all our sensations are subject. Will you easily persuade yourself that in a machine such as man, where everything is so closely linked, where all the organs act and react on each other, one of its parts, solid or fluid, can be vitiated with impunity for the others? Will you simply persuade yourself that the nature of the humours, the blood, the lymph, the capacity of the vessels of the whole body, the system of glands and nerves, the dura mater, the pie mater, the condition of the intestines, the heart, the lungs, the diaphragm, the kidneys, the bladder, the parts of generation, can vary without consequence for the brain and the cerebellum? You will persuade yourself that, whereas the tugging of a fibre is enough to provoke frightening spasms; the slowing or acceleration of the blood to bring delirium and lethargy; the inconsiderate loss of a few drops of sperm to weaken or increase activity ; the suspension or embarrassment of a secretion to throw one into a continuous state of malaise; the amputation or crumpling of two glands that seem to have nothing to do with intellectual functions to give voice or keep it, and to take away energy, courage, and almost metamorphose one sex into another? You will not, therefore, think that almost no man is born without some of these defects of organization, or that time, diet, exercise, pain and pleasure soon introduce them into us; and you will persist in the opinion either that the head will not be affected, or that this affection will be of no consequence for the combination of ideas, for attention, for reason and for judgment. Judge now how far you have remained from the solution of the problem you proposed; judge how strong my objection would be in the mouth of an educated physician who would fortify it with his speculative and practical knowledge.

When you asked that man, in order to be equally suited to all the operations of the mind, be commonly well organized, you made the vaguest, most unintelligible, most indeterminate request, since you were never able to include the condition of the cerebellum, nor that of the brain, nor that of the diaphragm, nor that of any of the other parts of the body. One man shows me today the most beautiful colors, stoutness, a lively eye, an athletic constitution, and tomorrow I am informed of his death; another, weak, delicate, pale, thin, exhausted, seems to me to have one foot in the grave, and lives for many years, without complaining of any infirmity.

Page 225 - Any man accustomed to the finer points of chicanery has difficulty getting back to the first principles of law.

Say any man in general, and do not regret the loss of those whom the habit of the forms of the palace and the subtleties of chicanery have swaddled. Rid them of these swaddling clothes, and they will no longer be chicaners, without becoming greater publicists as a result; they will be nothing.

If they had had any elevation of soul, any breadth of spirit, any feeling for the general good, they would either not have embraced the profession of quibbler, or they would have become disgusted with it.

If the spider doesn't stop spinning webs, it's because it's a spider.

You're either born strong or weak. All things being equal, the man born strong is less inclined to the justice that binds the nervous arms, than the weak whom it protects and whose strength it makes whole.

But if strength is combined with a deep sense of justice, these two contradictory elements will give rise to heroism.

I made this remark to show that love or dislike for certain virtues has its source in organization.

Undoubtedly, a man in whom the fluids are acrid, caustic and burning, the seed reservoirs vast and deep, the fibers lining the urethral canal highly sensitive, the organic movement of the generative parts frequent, rapid and tenacious, will be able to practice continence ; But will the constant exercise of this virtue be as easy for him, if he lives in a warm climate, if he feeds on succulent foods, if he drinks delicious wines, as for him in whom the liquors are indolent, the secretions weak, the fiber soft, and who lives in a rainy atmosphere, who observes a frugal diet, who eats only roots and drinks only nenufar?

Conclude, then, that there is an organization, a diet, a climate that is unsuitable for certain virtues, and highly favorable to certain vices, and that these same causes, which have so much influence on temperament and character, have scarcely less on the qualities of the mind.

SECTION III.

SECOND PART OF THE FIRST VOLUME.

Chance causes inequality of mind; desire causes the superiority of one man over another; every discovery, every new idea, favors chance. These are all random general propositions.

A man occupies himself with physics, anatomy, mathematics, history: the outcome of some of his studies leads him to a conjecture that experience justifies: and the author calls this chance.

Descartes, an algebraist and geometer, realized that the signs of algebra could also represent numbers, lines, surfaces and solids, and that the expression of an algebraic truth could be rendered or translated into figures: he invented the application of algebra to geometry; and the author calls this chance.

Leibnitz and Newton imagine at the same time that the signs of algebra can also express the ratio of two finite quantities, or the vanishing ratio of these two quantities, and they publish the method of differential and integral calculus; and the author calls this chance.

Newton, sitting in a garden, sees fruit detach from the tree and fall; he ponders the cause of gravity, and suspects that the force which precipitates the gravel towards the earth's re-entry, holds celestial bodies in their orbits: he compares this idea with astronomical observations, and discovers the law of the universe; and the author calls this chance.

Galileo sees bodies fall, and realizes that their speed increases with each instant: he investigates the law of this acceleration by experiment, and discovers that the spaces covered in equal times are like the sequence of odd numbers; and the author calls this chance.

Rœmer assumes that the speed of light is not instantaneous; he searches the tables for the times of immersion and emersion of a satellite of Jupiter; he observes and realizes that the satellite can still be seen when it should be hidden behind the planet, and that it cannot yet be seen when it should have emerged from it: from which he concludes that the difference between the immersion or emersion and the appearance or disappearance of the satellite, is the precise length of time that light takes to travel from the satellite or Jupiter to the earth; and the author calls this chance.

And as chances are made equally for all men commonly well organized, the author concludes from this the equality of minds: a method for making people of genius. In truth, it's pitiful.

Tell him: It's nature, it's organization, it's purely physical causes that prepare the man of genius; it's moral causes that make him blossom; it's assiduous study, it's acquired knowledge that leads him to happy conjectures; it's these conjectures verified by experience that immortalize him. He will reply: As for me, I see in all this only a chain of coincidences, the first of which is his existence and the last his discovery; and there are no men commonly well organized who were not born with the aptitude for the same fate and the same illustration.

This vision consoles me and must console many others; for what man is foolish enough to be humbled by a predilection of chance? What man can fail to see himself as a man of genius, if chance so wills? Helvétius, you're smiling, and why are you smiling? I am not commonly well, I am well organized; I have sense, I have knowledge, I have the habit of meditation. I would like nothing better than to enjoy great esteem during my lifetime and to leave an illustrious name after my death; a violent desire to discover, to invent, interrupts my sleep at night, pursues me during the day; all I lack is a happy chance, I'm waiting for it; it's true it's been about fifty years, without it having come; but who told you it wouldn't come?... You're smiling again, and you're right.

If it happens to anyone other than a D'Alembert, a La Grange, an Euler, or some other geometer of the same strength to perfect the calculation of fluxions, I swear to believe in Helvétius and his chance; but I'm not risking anything.

CHAPTER I.

Page 2. - Our memory is the crucible of blowers.

Yes, but throw into a crucible, without choice or plan, various materials taken at random; and on an attempt that will yield you something useful, a hundred times, a thousand times you will have lost your crucible, your time, your ingredients and your coal.

CHAPTER II.

Ibid. - An entirely unknown truth cannot be the object of my meditation.

We don't think about what we don't know, that's obvious; but in every science and every art, we know what has been done, what remains to be done, the obstacles to be overcome, the advantages to be perceived, the honor to be reaped, and we start from there to meditate and attempt experiments. What does chance have to do with it?

Ibid. - When I glimpse a truth, it has already been discovered.

It's the habitual occupation of my state that constantly brings me back to the discoveries to be made to bring it to perfection. As I dream of the different ways to successfully solve some of these problems, one presents itself to my mind, and this means is the effect of some new facets under which I have compared my object: it may be good or bad, I try it out. This is what Helvétius apparently means by glimpsing a truth. But what do we glimpse when we conjecture, when we ignore the end of our road, when the truth we seek is at the end of that road, when, tortuous or straight, we are uncertain whether we can follow it to the end, when in following it to the end we encounter only an illusion, its phantom?

As you become disillusioned with one deceptive means, you sometimes come up with another which you think is more solid, but which is no more so; a third which seduces you, and which when you try it out, you recognize as unsuccessful as the previous ones, and so on for many years, until you succeed or die from the effort.

This is what I call the history of errors or discoveries; and the former, of no use to science, would often show more sagacity on the part of the inventor.

Fable has hidden Truth at the bottom of a well so deep that not all eyes can see it. I lean the philosopher on the edge of this well; he looks: at first he sees only darkness; little by little this darkness seems to lose its thickness; he believes he glimpses the Truth: his heart leaps with joy, but soon he recognizes his error, what he took for the Truth was not. His soul withers, but he is not discouraged; he rubs his eyes, he redoubles his efforts; there comes a moment when he exclaims with transport: It's her!... and it is indeed, or it isn't. He doesn't look for her in the dark, he looks for her in the light. He's not a blind man groping around, he's a clear-sighted man who's thought long and hard about how best to use his eyes in different circumstances. He tries out these methods, and when he's convinced of their inadequacy, what does he do? Then he no longer looks at the bottom of the well, he looks inside himself; there he promises to discover both the different ways in which one can hide in a well, and the different tricks one can use to bring out the Truth that has withdrawn there.

From this we see that it is not to chance that one owes one's first attempt, but to a knowledge of the imperfections of one's art, a knowledge gained from study; and that it is no more to chance that one must attribute the means of discovery than the discovery itself.

Nothing is made by leaps and bounds in nature and the sudden and rapid flash of light that passes through the mind is linked to an earlier phenomenon with which we would recognize its connection, if we were not infinitely more anxious to enjoy its glow than to seek its cause. The fruitful idea, however bizarre it may be, however fortuitous it may seem, is not at all like the stone that detaches itself from the roof and falls on a person's head. The stone would strike any head equally exposed to its fall. This is not the case with the idea; and it is not indifferent to Fontaine, who is concerned with the perfection of new calculations, to meet D'Alembert or Clairaut, or some other geometer. A passer-by does not say to another passer-by: You stole my stone... and every day I hear one scientist say to another: You've stolen my idea. How many of them fall on deaf ears!

Certainly, it is to the heat of a conversation, an argument, a reading, a word, that we sometimes owe the first suspicion of a truth; but to whom does this suspicion come? To all men commonly well organized. By how many preliminaries has it been prepared!

Page 2. - When I glimpse an unknown truth, it has already been discovered.

The author has not considered that everything holds together in human understanding as well as in the universe, and that the most disparate idea that seems to come dazedly across my current meditation, has its very unravelled thread that links it either to the idea that occupies me, or to some phenomenon that takes place inside or outside of me ; that with a little attention I would unravel this thread and recognize the cause of the sudden approach and point of contact of the present idea and the occurred idea, and that the little jolt which awakens the insect lurking at a great distance in an obscure corner of the apartment and accelerates it near me, is as necessary as the most immediate consequence to the two premises of the tightest syllogism ; therefore that everything is chance or nothing; and that, either in the course of the events of our lives, or in the long sequence of our studies, by going back further and further, we never fail to arrive at an unforeseen fact, a trivial circumstance, an incident in appearance the most indifferent and perhaps in reality, because the impulse which would not have come to us by this shock would have been given to us by another. If that's what we meant, it wasn't worth it; if it's something else, it doesn't make sense. In the man who thinks, a necessary chain of ideas; in the man attached to such and such a profession, a necessary chain of such and such ideas. In the man who acts, a chain of incidents, the most insignificant of which is as constrained as the rising of the sun. A double necessity specific to the individual, a destiny woven from the origin of time to the moment I am now; and it is the momentary oblivion of these principles with which we are imbued that scatters a work with contradictions. One is a fatalist, and at every moment one thinks, speaks and writes as if one were persevering in the prejudice of liberty, a prejudice one has been lulled into, which has instituted the vulgar language one has stammered and continues to use, without realizing that it no longer suits one's opinions. We've become philosophers in our systems, and we're still people in our language.

Everything is done within us, because we are us, always us, and not for a minute the same.

Page 3. - Now, if we are indebted to chance for these first suspicions, and consequently for these discoveries, can we be sure that we don't still owe him the means to extend and perfect them?

And if I were to grant the one and deny the other; if I were to claim, to use your word, that there is infinitely more chance in invention than in perfection, would I be so wrong? Invention sometimes seems to fall from the sky; perfection seems more reflexive, and more the result of a perpetuity of one man's efforts added to the efforts of a predecessor, another, a third predecessor, all of whom have taken turns carrying the burden.

So many Ixions successively attached to the same wheel, so many Prometheus and so many vultures tearing them apart.

There are fortuitous experiences, no doubt about it; but to whom should they be best presented? To the craftsman. In whose hands should they be fruitful? In the hands of the educated man.

It is the more or less general usefulness, not the degree of sagacity of the inventor, that gives the invention its lustre.

Helvétius says it, and I prove it. Let a geometer mark three points on paper: let him suppose a certain law of attraction between these three points and seek their movements; his solution will be no more than an effort whose sensation will scarcely extend beyond one of the halls of the Academy. But the moment he said: One of these points is the Earth, the other the Moon, and the third the Sun... the Universe rang with his name.

Page 3. - There are reliable methods for training scientists: there are none for training men of genius.

If Helvétius had looked carefully, he would have seen that those who have been given the aptitude for science owe their erudition no less to chance than those who have been given the aptitude or organization for genius by nature owe their discoveries to it.

He would have seen that there is no more or no less method for making a scholar than for making a man of genius, without presupposing an organization peculiar to each of these states.

He would have seen that this presupposed organization, honors and rewards would multiply without number those kinds of players and happy events that the author calls chances.

He would have seen that, without this presupposed organization, all imaginable means would have been sterile.

What, then, is the importance of education? It is not at all to make the first commonly well-organized child do what his parents please, but to apply him constantly to the thing to which he is suited: to erudition, if he is endowed with a great memory; to geometry, if he easily combines numbers and spaces; to poetry, if he is recognized as having warmth and imagination; and so to the other sciences: and that the first chapter of a good treatise on education should be on how to know the child's natural dispositions.

CHAPTER III.

Page 6. - The inequality of minds comes less from the unequal sharing of the gifts of chance than from the indifference with which they are received.

- And where does this difference come from?

- From the difference in attention.

- And this different attention?

- Interest.

- And interest?

- From instruction.

- But instruction doesn't give interest; it sometimes destroys it.

- I include all kinds of encouragement in instruction.

- But there are a thousand examples of children who have been encouraged by every possible means to do nothing, and others who have been discouraged by every possible means from the thing they have done, sometimes well, sometimes badly or mediocrely, in spite of all the obstacles that have been thrown in their way.

There's something fishy about the beginning of this third chapter. Is it my fault or the author's? I don't know. Helvétius says: "If almost all objects considered with attention did not contain within them the seed of some discovery; if chance did not divide its gifts more or less equally, and did not offer to all objects from the comparison of which great and new ideas might result, the mind would be almost entirely the gift of chance." I think I'd hear him better if he had said: "If chance shared his gifts equally, if he offered everyone, etc."

We receive the gifts of chance with indifference.

It's as if the art of discovery were a game in which one loses through one's own fault, and as if Newton's valet had been very wrong to let his master have the chance to experiment on light.

Helvétius says: It's chance that makes an author think about this or that subject.

You say: He's either a geometer, a metaphysician or a mechanic. That's his trade.

Helvétius says: It's chance that fixes the author's gaze on this or that point of science or art.

You say: Nothing is more natural and more ordinary than to attach ourselves to the places where the efforts of our predecessors have stopped, and to start from there to take a step forward.

A coincidence would be the case where Vaucanson was concerned with a eulogy, and Thomas with a machine.

Go to D'Alembert's or Fontaine's, and you'll find them busy perfecting integral calculus, looking for a way to sum absolutely, or by some quick and easy approximation, an equation of a renitent form. Go to Bezout's house and ask him what he's doing. He'll tell you he's tormented by the general solution of equations of all degrees.

Helvétius says that it's by chance that we find the thing we're looking for.

You say that temptation is always preceded by a certain sequence of reasoning or systematic ideas to be verified by experience.

The only chance that exists between two men who are more or less equally skilful is that one, better led than the other, discovers what they were both equally capable of discovering. Peter runs as well as John, but John has unfortunately beaten him to the punch.

When Newton was asked how he discovered the system of the world, he didn't answer: by chance; but he did answer: by thinking about it a lot. Another might have added: and that he was him.

I know, like Bezout, where the progress of analysis has stopped; but if we deal with the same problem together, it's a thousand to one that he'll be the one to solve it, when it's a question of my life, and I'd give it a thousand times more attention than he would.

Helvétius says: There is no man driven by the ardent desire for glory who does not always distinguish himself more or less in the art or science he cultivates... Let him say it, it's not true; he speaks against experience.

Helvétius says: Between two men who are equally jealous of becoming famous, it is chance that decides... Let him say it; this jealousy can agitate the inept more violently than the man of genius; and: "I'd like to make a great discovery" is a very ordinary thing for a fool to say.

Helvétius says: Chance still presides over the choice of objects... Let him say it. Everyone is at his job, everyone's eyes are on the same side. One sees, because he has good eyes and his gaze is right; the other doesn't see, either because he has bad eyes or because he looks the wrong way. And the moment when the former sees best is not always the one when he kills himself looking, it's when he's tired of useless restraint, and lets his shallow, careless gaze wander over an object of which he's almost disgusted.

He who is all in one way sees only that way. He who hovers, as it were, above the object, sees several roads that can lead him there. There are circumstances where great attention concentrated on one point is harmful, and where a vague gaze is more useful.

Page 7. - The seeds of discoveries presented to all by chance are sterile, if attention does not fertilize them.

But is attention alone enough to fertilize them?

CHAPTER IV.

Page 8. - Your comparison of men to merchants is brilliant, but is it fair? It seems to me that there is an appalling struggle between all those who pursue the same career, and that this outrageous emulation goes as far as injustice and hatred. The sea is the same. All try to make discoveries; but one walks at random, he has only a bad pilot, he lacks a compass, his ship is a bad sailboat.

There is not one who does not know that the path to fortune, honor and wealth is the same.

Page 8. - There are few Colombs; and on the seas of this world, only jealous of honors, places, credit and riches, few men embark for the discovery of new truths.

I'm not surprised, especially if your system is true. All our thoughts, all our labors, all our views resolve themselves in the last analysis to sensual pleasures. So what does the man do who takes gold and disdains discovery? He goes straight to the point, he's wise. Why do you want him to make a long circuit to arrive at a near term?

The author was on the open sea before, now he's in the depths of the forest where a thousand swirl and swirl without discovering anything. The man of genius has opened the path, the multitude smoothes it out: this is the class of classical authors, a class that is not prized enough, clear minds, fair minds that make science common.

Page 9. - What is the need for glory? It is the need for pleasure; in any country where glory ceases to be representative of it, the citizen is indifferent to glory.

Yes, the citizen in general.

Only in old age do we feel as the author does. The spectacle of the illustrious man dying of hunger is constantly exposed to the eyes of children by sensible fathers. Unhappy man, what do you want to do? It's uncertain whether you'll go on to glory, and you're running straight into misery... These are the words our homes resound with, but they hardly convert anything but mediocre children; the others let their parents say it, and go where nature calls them. All that the author adds is suitable only for those who are not truly called.

SECTION IV.

CHAPTER I.

Page 13. - At the moment when a child detaches itself from its mother's side and opens the doors of life, it enters without ideas or passions.

Without ideas, it's true, but with a disposition to conceive, compare and retain some with more taste and ease than others. Without exercised passions, I ignore it; without passions ready to develop, I deny it; with an equal inclination to all kinds of passions, I still deny it; with an inclination to all kinds of passions, I think I could deny it. There are men who have never known avarice. It is rare not to have a dominant passion, rarer to be equally dominated by two; just as rare that a dominant passion should not have been detected by a watchful eye in the first years of life, long before the age of reason. A sneaky child shows himself sneaky at six months; a child shows himself lively or clumsy, impatient or quiet, insensitive or angry, sad or cheerful. Anything else the author adds would suggest that he has never observed children.

Page 14. - Has it ever been noticed that a certain disposition in the nerves, fluids or muscles constantly gives the same way of thinking?

Yes, we have. It is on the disturbance of this habitual way of thinking in the state of health, and on the new symptoms or the new turn it takes, that part of the doctor's prognosis is based.

Does mind change body?

No, the moral does not change the physical, but it constrains it, and this continuous constraint ends up robbing it of all its primitive and natural energy.

We inspire boldness in a pusillanimous child, moderation in a violent child, circumspection in a giddy child; we teach him these things just as we teach him to moderate his cries in pain: he suffers, but he no longer complains.

Does nature remove certain fibers from the brain of some to add them to that of others? Does a tutor straighten a hunchback's back?

You reason about the head as well as the feet, about brain fibers as well as leg bones; yet these are very different things. What nature has done well, a bad habit can spoil, a lack of exercise can destroy, just as both can rectify what she has done badly. The surgeon whose soul is troubled and whose hand wavers in the first operations, hardens and ceases to quiver; the doctor's bowels cease to torment, in the long run : both see the convulsions and hear the cries of the nephritic without being moved; the midwife soon pulls the child from the womb of the laboring mother, without feeling the slightest pity; the butcher, by dint of dipping his hands in the blood of animals, sees human blood flow without horror. Bloody spectacles and public torments end up making a whole nation atrocious, witness the Roman women who condemned a bad gladiator to death.

There is not a word in this entire chapter that reason and experience do not contradict.

We love each other in every country...

It's true; but each individual in a country loves in his own way.

CHAPTER II.

Page 16. - The character of peoples changes; but when is this change most noticeable? In moments of revolution, when people suddenly pass from freedom to slavery. Then, from being proud and bold, a people becomes weak and pusillanimous.

This is frowned upon; it's not the way things are done. Then there remains in the depths of souls a feeling of freedom that gradually fades, a feeling that the tyrants' ministers recognize in themselves and respect in the new slaves. These are the children of tyrants who dare everything, and the subjugated children of free men who suffer everything. I can attest to this in the terrors and guards that surrounded the scoundrel Maupeou as he crossed the capital on his way to the palace.

Page 17. - Does a prince usurp unbounded authority over his people? He is sure to change their character.

You are mistaken. This is not the work of a single despot; he begins it, and his successors, aided by the cowardice of their fathers, carry it out on their children. The subjugated fathers, by their example and their speeches, teach their children the role of the slave: unceasingly they say to those who impatiently wear their chains and shake them: "Beware, my son, you will lose yourself..." Morality is depraved, even in the works of philosophers. Around a tiger's cave, it's security, not revolt, that is preached. When I read in Saâdi: He is very wise who knows how to hide his secret from his friend, it is useless to tell me in which country and under which government he was writing.

Page 18. - Nothing is better," said the King of Prussia in a speech to the Berlin Academy, "than arbitrary government under just, humane and virtuous princes.

And it is you, Helvétius, who praise this maxim of a tyrant! The arbitrary government of a just and enlightened prince is always bad. His virtues are the most dangerous and surest of seductions: they insensitively accustom a people to love, respect and serve his successor, whoever he may be, wicked and stupid. It deprives the people of the right to deliberate, to will or not to will, even to oppose his will, when he orders the good; yet this right of opposition, however foolish it may be, is sacred: without it, the subjects resemble a herd whose claim is scorned, under the pretext that it is being led into fat pastures. By ruling according to his own pleasure, the tyrant commits the greatest of crimes. What characterizes a despot? Is it goodness or badness? Not at all; these two notions do not enter into his definition. It is the extent, not the use, of the authority he arrogates to himself. One of the greatest misfortunes that could befall a nation would be two or three reigns of a just, gentle, enlightened but arbitrary power: the people would be led by happiness to the complete oblivion of their privileges, to the most perfect slavery. I don't know if a tyrant and his children ever thought of this formidable policy, but I have no doubt that it would have succeeded. Woe betide those subjects in whom any shadow is cast on their freedom, even by the most apparently praiseworthy means. These ways are all the more disastrous for the future. This is how we fall into a very sweet sleep, but into a sleep of death, during which patriotic sentiment is extinguished, and we become strangers to the government of the State. Give the English three Elizabeths in succession, and they will be the last slaves of Europe.

Page 19 - Men are therefore born with either no disposition at all, or dispositions to all the vices and virtues to the contrary.

All of the above is true, but the conclusion is flawed. Whether man is born with a disposition or no disposition at all to all the vices and virtues, that's what I don't know. It's the doctor I'd consult on this point, rather than all the books in the world. If I were to believe any testimony, it would be that of the fathers of many families; nothing is more common than to hear them say: "This one has always been gentle, kind and frank; that other one cunning, wicked and hidden..." and to back up their speeches with traits of character from their early childhood.

Ibid. - At first, foreigners perceive the French to be of the same mind and character.

Among the various reasons for this phenomenon, Helvétius may well have overlooked the main one. This general and common physiognomy is a consequence of their extreme sociability; they are coins whose imprint has been worn away by continuous friction. No nation resembles a single family more; a Frenchman is more numerous in his city than ten Englishmen, than fifty Dutchmen, than a hundred Moslems in theirs: the same man, on the same day, can be found at court, in the city, in the country, in an academy, in a circle, at a banker's, a notary's, a public prosecutor's, a lawyer's, a great lord's, a merchant's, a worker's, in church, at the show, at a girl's, and everywhere equally free and familiar; it's as if he hadn't left home and had only changed apartments. The other capitals are heaps of houses, each with its own owner. Paris seems to be one big common house, where everything belongs to everyone, right down to the women; so there's no condition that doesn't borrow something from the condition above it; they all touch at a few points. The court reflects on the great and the great reflect on the small. The result is a luxury of imitation, the most disastrous of all: a luxury that is an ostentation of opulence in a small number, a mask of misery in almost all the others. The result is an assimilation that blurs all ranks: an assimilation that is increased by a continual influx of foreigners to whom we become accustomed to being polite, here by custom, there by interest. Anyone who has been with us for seven or eight months and has not found us to be such, or has not bothered to see us, or has brought with him some off-putting defect that has kept us from his trade, or is stubbornly prejudiced in some way that prevents him from observing us impartially. The first acquaintance may be difficult to make, especially for a foreign woman; but the first acquaintance we make quickly leads to many more.

Page 20 - Whatever our national uniformity, one always discovers some difference between the characters and minds of individuals; but it takes time.

And this is perhaps one of the reasons why comedy is so difficult to do among us.

CHAPTER III.

Ibid. - The most imperious man trembles in the lion's den.

That is, the angriest man is not angry in the arms of his mistress. What does this prove?

That the most voluptuous man, when his strength is exhausted, may feel disgust for women. What does this prove?

Page 21. - A tree that is kept bent for a long time will lose its elasticity.

I believe it, I even believe that there is no physical quality in the animal, in bronze or iron, that cannot be destroyed; not a moral quality in man that cannot be overcome by long constraint.

All physical qualities carried to excess are lost. Bend a foil to the hilt and it will never straighten again. Take an iron rod, expose it to the fire until it melts, and then throw it into fresh water; I have no doubt that this repeated operation will deprive it of the property of expanding with heat and contracting with cold. Bend two springs against each other, and they will eventually stop squeezing.

Would the author advise putting this violence to education? Are there very few examples of those who have been broken by a long servitude contrary to their character, whose health it has ruined and whose life it has shortened?

If instead of bending this foil to the hilt, you fencer it lightly, far from destroying its elasticity you will increase it. The same is true of temper: momentary constraint will embitter it.

The great return from court more imperious and insolent.

You can teach a bear to dance, but a dancing bear is a very unhappy animal. I'll never be taught to dance.

There are men who never take the spirit of their state. Malherbe was gruff in his study and gruff in the king's antechamber.

If a child is born indifferent to any vice, any virtue, any talent, education must be one for all.

Answer, Monsieur Helvétius, should all children be raised in the same way?

- More or less.

- And why more or less and not strictly?

In the cradle, in the school, in every state of society, at court, in the palace, in the church, in war, in his workshop, in his store, each individual has his own character.

- This is because education has not been the same.

- If it had been, the same diversity would still exist, despite all the circumstances, all the lessons and all the incidents of chance.

One of the symptoms of a fatal illness is a change of character.

Page 22. - Why look at each character as the effect of a particular organization, when we can't determine what that organization is?

Open the medical textbooks to the chapters on temperament, and you'll find the specific organization of each character.

When we see something, we don't have to explain it in order to admit it.

CHAPTER IV.

Page 23. - Self-love is permanent and unalterable.

But does it have the same energy in everyone? Does it not vary? Does it not change? The only point on which I will not dispute is that everyone loves himself as much as it is possible for everyone to love himself. But two men, yes, just two men reduced by nature, experience or institution to the same dose of self-love, would be the most astonishing of all prodigies.

CHAPTER V.

Page 24. - Are there men without desires, men insensible to the love of power? Yes, but there are too few of them to have any regard for it.

But their existence, which you admit to, perhaps a little too lightly, at least proves the prodigious diversity of this feeling. It's a ratio that increases from zero to a number whose limit I don't know.

Page 25 - If eloquence degenerates under despotic governments, it is less because it remains unrewarded than because it occupies itself with frivolous objects and is constrained. In Greece, Demosthenes spoke to the people about the salvation of the State. What would he talk about in Paris? The dissolution of a mismatched marriage.

CHAPTER VI.

Page 27. - The work is excellent; it is published, and the public does not pay its debt.

Helvétius misrepresents everything. This is almost without example, and I have more often seen mediocre or even bad works applauded than excellent or good works ignored or decried.

In the first moment, the beauties are spoken of lightly, and the minor faults are emphasized. The praise of the beauties is for the author, the criticism of the faults is for oneself. Then it becomes a subject of discussion and dispute, it leads to schism, and so much the better. In the heat of the schism, one exaggerates both good and bad. Finally, silence falls, impartiality is established, and the final sentence is pronounced. The author is dissatisfied, because he has promised himself more success than he is getting; because the small laurel leaf he is awarded does not compensate him for the trouble he has taken; because this same reward has been too long in coming, and he has grown cold.

Page 28. - Early youth knows no envy.

God be praised! I have remained quite young. I am more interested in the perfection of another's work than in the perfection of my own; my own success touches me less than the success of my friend; I respond with all my strength to the mark of esteem I receive from the one who consults me. Why should I be saddened by the applause he receives? I secretly reap my share. I have only ever been hurt by a kind of little falsehood, which is to have so rarely the advantage of pointing out to the author either a flaw or a beauty on which he has not gained speed with you: what you tell him, he knew. For forgetting the pages I have sown in several works, I am accustomed to meeting and forgiving him.

Page 30 - Who can boast of having courageously praised genius?

Answer. Me, me.

I believe I have examined myself well and have never suffered from the success of others, not even when I hated. I've sometimes said: "He's a clown, but this clown has written a fine poem, a fine eulogy; I'm glad, it's always one more fine work."

What's the important thing? Is the sublime thing mine or is it done? We're short-sighted. And what does it matter what name is printed at the head of your book or engraved on your tombstone? Will you read your epitaph?

My friends, you are as childish as Mme du Barry, who, proud of her superb carriage, used to say: Mon Dieu, que je voudrais bien se voir passer!

Ibid. - Who hasn't added a "but" to her praise?

My but came like envy's, with the difference that envy's but always fell on a defect, and mine fell on an omitted or missed beauty.

CHAPTER VIII.

Page 34. - Everything the author says here about the savage state may be true; but I am not. More civilized than he, I apparently have too much trouble getting naked or getting back into animal skin. Less strong than someone else, I can't enjoy this plea of strength, and I don't believe in it.

It seems to me that, before any social convention, if it happens to a savage to climb a tree and pick fruit from it, and another savage comes along and seizes the fruit and labor of the first, that savage will flee with his flight ; that by his flight he will reveal the consciousness of an injustice or an action which must excite resentment; that he will confess himself punishable and that he will give himself, in force, the shameful name which we use in society. It seems to me that the robbed will be indignant, will hasten to come down from the tree, will pursue the thief and will be equally conscious of the insult done to him. It seems to me that they will both have some idea of the property or possession taken by work: without having explained themselves, it seems to me that between these two savages there is a primitive law which characterizes actions, and of which written law is only the interpreter, the expression and the sanction. The savage has no words to designate what is just and unjust; he cries out, but is his cry devoid of meaning? is it no more than the cry of an animal? But man is not a beast, and this difference must not be overlooked when judging his actions. Would it be right to conclude from man to man by comparing animal to animal, eagle to dove, lion to deer, shark to sea bream, or even eagle to eagle or deer to deer? I'm not pronouncing, I'm questioning. I wish I didn't allow the wicked to appeal from the eternal law of nature to the created and conventional law; I wish I didn't allow him to say to others and to himself: "After all, what am I doing?

Page 36. - Justice presupposes established laws.

But does it not presuppose some prior notion in the mind of the legislator, some idea common to all those who subscribe to the law? Otherwise, when it was said to them: You shall do this, because it is just; you shall not do that, because it is unjust... they would have heard only a vain noise, to which they would have attached no meaning.

CHAPTER IX.

Page 37. - Despite man's alleged love of justice, there is no Asiatic despot who does not commit injustice, and who does so without remorse.

Among these Asiatic despots, there have been a few whose goodness, humanity and benevolence have been praised. If the ferocious beasts who succeeded them in arbitrary power hear the praise of these qualities with contempt, I'll believe they commit injustice without remorse.

But if tyrants are wicked without remorse, where do their terrors come from, where do so many precautions for their safety come from? It seems to me as difficult for the oppressor to be without remorse as it is for the oppressed to be without resentment.

Does man think of a lion who attacks him as of a tyrant who crushes him? No. What difference then does he make between these malefactors, if it does not derive from some natural prerogative, some confused idea of humanity and justice? But if the persecuted has this idea, why should the persecutor lack it? If the persecutor doesn't have it when his throat is cut, why would he demand it when his throat is cut? I'm not pronouncing, I'm questioning.

Page 38. - It is fear and weakness that make respect for the law of nations.

I know what the conduct of civilized nations is among themselves; I am only worried about the opinion they have of themselves, and the name they give themselves in the secret court of their conscience. A brigand speaks as he pleases, but he does not feel as he would like.

CHAPTER X.

Page 41. - The abuse of power is linked to power, as the effect is to the cause.

Titus, Trajan and Marcus Aurelius refute this evil maxim.

The first origin of the great idea that men attach to the word force... When man had to fight the tiger for the forest, force, the only thing necessary for this conquest, was too useful not to be highly valued. When it came to felling the forest, clearing the plains and cultivating the land, strength, almost the only thing needed for this work, was too useful not to be highly valued. When the societies were closed, the strength that was so advantageous in battle had to command respect. Esteem and respect increased when strength accompanied courage, two qualities that formed the character of the Hercules, the Jason, the Theseus, the heroes whose names will never be uttered without admiration, even in centuries when there was no difference between the illustrious character and the brigand. The spirit of conquest would still be in honor today, if the philosopher, or the friend of humanity, had not debased it.

CHAPTER XI.

Page 44. - In a despotic state, what respect would we have for an honest man?

The same as for a virtuous woman in a country lost to gallantry.

Such is the imposing authority of virtue in all parts of the earth, under all kinds of governments, that the rarer it is, the more veneration we have for it. It dies of cold and hunger, but it is praised.

What terrible truths have virtuous men, whose memory will never perish in the homeland of despotism, not had the courage to make the despot hear, almost always at the risk of their lives, often with impunity? Often it has happened that the voice of a good man has astonished and suspended the ferocity of these tigers.

Page 47. - One of the strongest proofs that men do not love justice for justice's sake, is the baseness with which the kings themselves honored injustice in the person of Cromwel.

You are mistaken. The kings who honored injustice in his person were the first to blush at it; all honest men turned a blind eye to it; all those who were able to explain it freely spoke of it as you do.

What has been said above about republican government seems to me to be entirely true; but since democratic government presupposes the concert of wills, and the concert of wills presupposes men gathered together in a fairly narrow space, I believe that there can only be small republics, and that the security of the only kind of society that can be happy will always be precarious.

CHAPTER XII.

Page 49 - No matter what you say, you don't really despise someone you don't dare despise to his face.

This is not true. Will I get killed by a spadassin, telling him he's a rascal?

Pages 49-50. - If, in centuries of oppression, virtue sometimes shone brightest; if, when Thebes and Rome were groaning under tyranny, the intrepid Pelopidas and the virtuous Brutus were born and armed, it was because the scepter was still uncertain in the hands of the tyrant; it was because virtue could still pave the way to greatness and power.

Despite tyranny, corruption, baseness and the uselessness of virtue, virtuous men are born everywhere, living and dying by their principles. It must be said that they are rare.

I feel that this work saddens me and that it takes away my sweetest illusions. With the lantern of this Diogenes, I can hardly find a good man, and I would search in vain for a happy people.

Ibid. - What esteem would the court of a Phocas have for the character of a Léontine?

Either I'm very much mistaken, or the greatest. It's in the lion's den that it's beautiful to brave it.

At the theater, I admire the good man, both in plays drawn from the history I know and in plays whose backgrounds are pure invention and whose names are fictitious. Three quarters of the audience who marvel or weep are ignorant and completely unfamiliar with Brutus, Caesar, Sallustus, Titus Livius and Tacitus. I don't know what impression an Asiatic would receive from the spectacle of these great Greek or Roman souls; and it's a slight pronouncement to say that he wouldn't be moved by them, while we sit on the same bench next to the courtier who comes to admire Burrhus, after having played the role of Narcissus at Court.

A villain cannot despise virtue; I don't even know if he can hate it.

CHAPTER XIII.

Page 51. - Most people in Europe honor virtue in speculation: they despise it in practice.

I think not.

Page 52 - It seems to me that there is much wit and little truth in this whole page. I consult myself sincerely and it seems to me that the superiority of an ancient character has never humiliated me, and that I have never ridiculed the heroism of one of my fellow citizens. This is because, when I go to a show, I leave all my interests and passions at the door, only to pick them up again on my way out. Not so when I go to church to hear a sermon.

It's a very respectable place for a wicked man to go and forget for three hours what he is. I don't know if the magistrate knows how useful it is.

Page 53 - Aeneas is a fairer character than Achilles. Why do we admire the latter?

Aeneas' character is flat, while Achilles' is sublime. The people believe him

Impiger, iracundus, inexorabilis, acer.

Jura neget sibi nata, nihil non arroget armis.

HORAT. De Arte poet, v. 121-122.

Anyone who knows him from the poet who painted him will hardly find any of these faults. Achilles is great, Achilles is just; he respects the laws, he is brave without ostentation, he knows friendship, he knows tenderness, he is not hard-hearted, he is not inflexible. It was he who said to the ambassadors who came to snatch Briseis, the prize of victory: Come, envoys of the gods, it is not you who offend me. It was he who said to his servants: Throw a carpet over this corpse, so that the sight of this unfortunate father will not be distressed. It was he who, after the death of Patroclus, went off at night to lie on the sands of the sea and mingle his plaintive voice with the tumult of the waves.

I return to the effect of spectacles. Ideas of interest obsess me and trouble me in society, but they disappear in the region of hypotheses; there, I am magnanimous, equitable, compassionate, because I can be so without consequence.

Nothing is more common than a spectator at the theater, or a reader with a book in his hand; nothing more rare than an honest citizen.

CHAPTER XIV.

Page 54. - There is one phenomenon, constant in nature, to which Helvétius has not paid attention, and that is that strong souls are rare, that nature makes almost only common beings; that this is the reason why moral causes so easily subjugate organization. Whatever the public or private education, whatever the governments and legislation, except in times of enthusiasm, which is and can only be a temporary spring, the multitude will show you nothing but a mixture of goodness and badness.

Helvétius had a lot more Platonism in his head than he realized.

Folly consists in preferring the interest of a moment to the happiness of one's life; passion sees no further than its nose. By what means can the number of madmen and passionate men be reduced?

There were just as many wicked and mad men in Athens and Rome as there were in Paris.

- And great men?

- I think they were less rare, and that's what I think the excellence of legislation boils down to. For the people, i.e. the multitude, it remains the same everywhere.

The mad and the wicked are with us, we see them and the number seems infinite. Socrates and Cato counted as many in their time.

A whole nation from which we are separated by a long interval of time is reduced in our minds to a small number of famous names handed down to us by history. We are unlikely to believe that we could take a step through the streets of Athens without bumping into an Aristides, just as our nephews will believe that we could take a step through Paris without bumping into a Malesherbes or a Turgot.

Page 55 - A man's only love in virtue is the wealth and esteem it brings him.

In general, this is true; in detail, nothing could be further from the truth.

CHAPTER XV.

Page 56 - Men end up believing the opinions they are forced to publish.

Nothing is more contrary to the effect attributed to persecution than this maxim: Sanguis martyrum semen Christianorum. How many heads are intoxicated by the vapor of martyrs' blood!

Ibid. - What reasoning cannot do, violence does.

I know of nothing more contrary to experience.

Ibid. - Intolerance in monarchs is always the effect of their love for power. Not to think like them is to put a limit on their authority.

This is a hollow idea that has never crossed anyone's mind.

Page 59 - Once the strong have spoken, the weak are silenced, dumbed down and stop thinking.

This is not what happens. The moment the strong man has ordered silence, the weak man's fury to speak takes over.

It takes a long time to dumb down an enlightened nation. We've been working on it here for a long time, and it seems to me that the task is not very far advanced.

Page 60 - Helvétius, an outraged admirer of the King of Prussia, did not suspect that he was painting his administration line for line.

CHAPTER XXII.

In this chapter, the author recapitulates his paradoxes with a fearlessness that astonishes me. Here, I realized that we had retained all the vicious consequences, none of the proofs, nothing of this long sequence of new, piquant, strongly expressed truths, of these subtle observations by which we had been led. Of this defect which grieves me, the mediocre minds which always make the great number, and envy, from which the author claims that nobody is perfectly exempt, will use it successfully to lower the price of the work and stop its usefulness; but time will put it back in its place.

There is more real substance in one of these chapters than in the fifteen volumes of Nicole; it is more linked, more followed than Montaigne; and Charron has neither his boldness nor his color.

It's a veritable system of experimental morality, and all we have to do is restrict the conclusions a little, which any ordinary mind can do.

And why quibble with this author? After all, aren't the means he proposes the best that can be employed to multiply the number of good and great men in a nation?

CHAPTER XXIII.

Page 87. - Experience teaches that the fear of the rod, the whip or an even lighter punishment is enough to endow a child with the attention required for the study of reading and languages.

Experience teaches just the opposite; and I've seen children cruelly flayed when they didn't progress one step further in reading and language learning.

Ibid. - If the study of their own language generally seems less painful to children than the study of geometry, it's because...

- That's because it's not true. There is hardly a child who does not succeed in geometry, and just as few who do not succeed in the study of language on principle.

CHAPTER XXIV.

Page 89. - The stupid inhabitants of Kamschatka are extremely industrious at making clothes.

And how did this industry come about? Is it the product of a year, a lustre, two or three centuries? These prodigies are not the work of one man; they are the result of several generations of men successively occupied with the perfection of the same art, from the manufacture of cloth to that of the fabrics that fill us with wonder; it is over the course of a few thousand years that a long succession of stupid people have tormented themselves in Kamschatka to get to where they are today. I'll be surprised if a nervous arm lifts an enormous mass of lead, but if a multitude of men divide this mass between them, and each of them carries one or two ounces, it will no longer be a tour de force.

NOTES.

Page 97, no. 14. - Why does affability make merit bearable? It's because it makes it a little contemptible.

That's not what I mean. On the contrary, it seems to me that arrogant merit is rigorously debated, and that affable merit is praised.

Page 99, no. 24. - It is from the moment that the multiplied men were forced to cultivate the earth, that they felt the necessity of assuring the cultivator both his harvest and the property of the field he plowed.

So cultivation founded the right of ownership? And why? Because it's hard work. Are hunting and fishing less so? How could force, which steals everything that suits it, have failed to recognize its injustice when it seized the fish another had caught, or the deer he had killed? Without this preliminary admission of conscience, how could men have consented to laws? The first legislator undoubtedly took as his starting point a fact that contained the fundamental axiom of all morality: Do not do to others what you do not want done to you. If you answer the former, then he had some notion of justice prior to the law; if you answer the latter, you're talking obvious nonsense.

- The first laws emanated from the common interest of all, not from any idea of justice.

- But how would interest have brought about the concert of wills, if each individual had not conceived that it was right to do for all what all agreed to do for him? I always question, I never pronounce.

Page 100, no. 27. - Aristotle's classification of brigandage as a different kind of hunting makes me laugh. I am tempted to strike from the ranks of the wise a legislator who is so alien to any sense of humanity as to defend theft and injustice within three or four miles, and permit it beyond.

Page 102, n°29. - The much-vaunted love of fairness is therefore neither natural nor common to men.

Love, yes; but knowledge? for feeling, knowing and practicing are quite different things. I agree that the strong oppress the weak, when they are not held back by fear. What I find hard to conceive is that he is neither aware of his injustice, nor remorseful for his action, that he is sincerely convinced that he is using a legitimate right and that he would be a fool not to use it. As far as I'm concerned, I can't go back to that ancient state of stupefaction, when man had neither the ideas nor the language to articulate this right. Was there ever a time when man could be confused with beast? I don't think so: he was always a man, i.e. an animal combining ideas. But it was not the time when the violent and strong man addressed the first occupant with the energetic and urgent eloquence you attribute to him. He could not have said it better if he had studied rhetoric at the Collège Royal for two years, and philosophy for three or four years under Hobbes. To extinguish any notion of justice in him, you assume he's as stupid as a tiger; and to make him prove his right of the strongest, you make him as talkative as Carneades. It doesn't get any better.

Page 104, no. 32. - The more enlightened a nation is, the more it lends itself to the demands of fair government.

And there's more: these demands must be revoltingly unjust for it to refuse them.

The life of a sovereign is exposed only among a barbaric people; there, he is strangled or stabbed in an instant.

So what does a despot do by dumbing down his subjects? He bends trees, which end up breaking his brains as he rises.

Page 105, n°38. - A nation where vice was honored and virtue despised never was and never will be. The fewer honest women there are, the more honest women are revered; the more wicked people there are, the more good people are regarded: the horror of crime is all the less the more common the crime: the price of virtue is all the greater the rarer virtue is. When you hear a praise of probity, say that the nation is in the last degree of depravity, since the common duty of all is praised in an individual. Now is the time to say to your son or daughter: "Do you want to be pointed out like a phoenix? Don't have a lover, don't be a whore. - Do you want to be honored, called the only man? Don't be a knave to be hanged.

Vice has not always aroused the horror it deserved, but it has never won respect; the extreme of baseness is to excuse it.

Wherever the author speaks of religion, he substitutes the word papism for Christianity.

Thanks to this pusillanimous circumspection, posterity, not knowing what his true feelings were, will say: "What, this man who was so cruelly persecuted for his freedom of thought, believed in the Trinity, in Adam's sin, in the Incarnation! "This is how the fear of priests has spoiled, spoils and will spoil all philosophical works; how it made Aristotle alternately attacker and defender of final causes; how it made him invent the double doctrine; and how it has introduced into modern works a disgusting mixture of incredulity and superstition.

I like a philosophy that is clear, neat and frank, as it is in the System of Nature and even more so in Common Sense.

I would have said to Epicurus: If you don't believe in the Gods, why relegate them to the intervals of the worlds?

The author of the System of Nature is not an atheist on one page, a deist on another: his philosophy is all of a piece. Our nephews won't quote him for and against, as the followers of all cults attack and defend each other with equally precise passages from their allegedly revealed books, where we find: My father and I are one; my father is greater than I; and whose authority is used in favor of the most contradictory opinions: a reproach made to the sacred authors, in heterodox productions where we notice the same defect in every line, with the difference that it is a little more permitted to man to bias than to the Holy Spirit.

One more observation, and I'll close the first volume. Helvétius says somewhere (I think on page 29): The wish of the mediocre man is to have no superior.

Helvétius, say of any man, that is in your principles; except only the superior man, who perhaps believes himself to be the only man.

Our most unlimited desires are reduced to keeping the advantages of our lot and invading the advantages of the lot of others; that's the value of this so common and so ridiculous saying: I would like to be in his place. Dissatisfied with the present and the past, there is no future we fear less than our own.

Before moving on to the next volume, I fancy reciting to Helvétius the story of some great discovery, and interweaving it with a few questions.

Some parents, who were neither poor nor rich, had several children; they were concerned with education, and to ensure the education of these children, they studied their natural dispositions... and does this sound crazy to you? They saw in the eldest of two boys a taste for reading and study. They sent him to a provincial college, where he distinguished himself, and from there to Paris, to university classes where his teachers could never overcome his disdain for the frivolities of scholasticism. He was given notebooks on arithmetic, algebra and geometry, which he devoured. Later he turned to more pleasurable studies, and enjoyed reading Homer, Virgil, Tasso and Milton, but always returning to mathematics, like an unfaithful husband, weary of his mistress, returns from time to time to his wife... Monsieur Helvétius, what is so wonderful and fortuitous about all this?

On walks, at home in the early hours of the morning, at night in insomnia, his habit was to dream idly about a few desperate questions, between which he preferred to square the circle. The lunulae of Hippocrates of Chio kept coming back to him, and he said to himself: It's as impossible for there to be a sterile truth in science as an isolated phenomenon in nature. Why didn't Hippocrates' discovery produce anything? Corollary of the equality of the square of the hypotenuse to the squares of the other two sides, another truth must be its own, and another truth the corollary of this one; and so on ad infinitum. I'm not examining whether he reasoned rightly or wrongly; but he didn't reason this way by chance.

One day, he wondered why Hippocrates' lunulae, being equal, were carrable together and separately; and why, being unequal, they were still carrable together, and no longer separately?

He calls d the difference between two unequal lunulae, and finds that any circular space terminated by any concave and convex circular arcs is carrable, whenever the convex arcs resolve into a sum of differences + n d, and the concave arcs into the same sum of differences, but negative - n d.

He realizes that this is the case for two equal lunulae carrable together and for each of them carrable separately, both giving + n d and - n d.

He realizes that this is the opposite case, when the two lunulae are unequal; one giving + n d and m d, and the other + m d and - n d.

I'm not guaranteeing the certainty of his logic, I'm just explaining the workings of his mind, where I can only see the common train of life.

He proposes to form a space terminated by determined concave and convex arcs that is equal to given rectilinear spaces + or - n d. This first step was not difficult.

He added another condition to this space, namely that it be composed of partial, transponible, mobile spaces, so that by addition, supposition or simple displacement, a new value of the whole or the remainder results, equal to given rectilinear spaces + or - q d, where q is greater or less than n.

He finds this space, or at least he thinks he has, and consequently a value of d in given rectilinear spaces, and the solution to the problem.

I ask Helvétius if he sees more luck here than in the execution of a finance project and the continuation of a trial at the Palais and the Châtelet? However, the story of this alleged discovery is the story of all real discoveries. If Helvétius answers me stubbornly: Chance, chance... I say: Let's erect altars to chance and place his name at the head of all works of genius.

If he admits that this is an aïiaire of logic, I'll insist and ask him if he believes any mind capable of this logic? If he answers yes, I will reply that there is perhaps not a man in the world capable of pronouncing on my young man's solution, without having examined it, since there is certainly not one in a position to demonstrate the possibility or impossibility of the second condition of space that he flatters himself with having found.

And then, after a serious story, a light-hearted one.

Jupiter had dined with the Galactophagus (these Galactophagus were not men; for, certainly, there were no men yet on the lonely, mute earth), and the father of the gods intended to make up for a frugal dinner with a good supper. In the meantime, whist was being played and quarrels were breaking out. Jupiter gets in a mood and shouts: "Shall we not serve? The gods sit down in an uproar, and Jupiter finds himself placed between his wife and Minerva, his daughter; the goddess of Wisdom had her father on her right and Momus on her left. Her father gave her very serious advice; for Jupiter is serious, even when drinking; and Momus, drunk or sober, always mad, shook his hand, pressed his knee and spouted nonsense. My daughter," Jupiter would say to her, "between the pear and the cheese, it's been about fifty-five and a half centuries since I gave birth to you; you're starting to grow up; why don't you get married? I don't like celibacy; all bachelors, male or female, are scoundrels. The more I examine you, the more I find you fit to make and bring up children well; you'll be a good wife and an excellent mother. Virginity is a very sterile virtue. Come, my child, promise me that one day you'll be bored with being a virgin..." And with that, the father of Minerva and the gods seized a large flask of ambrosia, filled his glass, Momus' and his daughter's, and said: "Here's to you, your first child, I want to be its godfather; and here's to me..." And then, addressing Momus: "And you, Momus, what do you think? That a virgin of five thousand years and more is very-ridiculous, isn't it true? But who are we going to marry her off to? And as they ran through the number of people they could give her as a husband, they drank the health of each god they named, and Minerva was at least halfway through her cup. All this health warmed Jupiter's and Momus' spirits, and Minerva left the table feeling a little unsettled in Olympus. It was getting late; the games were over, and each of the immortals was returning to his dormitory, when Momus, who was either following or preceding Minerva, or giving her his hand, I don't know which of the three; when Momus, I say, soiled the goddess' candlestick, rushed at her, and, as she struggled between his arms and cried out in a low voice: "But, Momus, are you mad? ... but you're not thinking of it... you're... If anyone could see us!.." the goddess of Wisdom let herself be childish. Until now, it had been believed that Minerva had remained a virgin; this is not true: half willingly, half by force, she was once raped. I, myself, have known her bastard very intimately, and he is a good friend of mine. When the modest goddess felt her bosom swell and her inflexible breastplate refuse to accommodate her expanding waistline, she became worried. Truth noticed this, questioned her and had no trouble getting her to confess her adventure. The point was to prevent a scandal, because if it got out, imagine the surprise and what the gods would say! Minerva, chaste Minerva! a prude! a devotee! To this end, Truth persuaded her to retire with her to the bottom of a well and wait there for the end of her gestation period.

- But did the gods not notice the absence of these two goddesses?

- No, Minerva imposed her presence on them; almost everything Truth said offended them; Olympus was all the more cheerful for it. Finally, the time came for Minerva to give birth, and it was Truth who served as her midwife and delivered her. From time to time, Momus would come to the edge of the well and call out to them: "Speak up, beautiful ladies; have you resolved to spend eternity in your hole? Where are you with your sad task?" Minerva replied: "Unworthy! scoundrel! it's done; go and get us a wet nurse..." Momus comes and goes with a fat, chubby girl, without reason, without care, laughing without knowing why, talking incessantly without knowing what she's saying. The child is given to her, and she takes it away. Momus and Minerva return to heaven, each on his own, and Truth remains at the bottom of her well, where she still is.

- And the bastard?

- I'd never finish telling you all about his various fortunes. Do you see this enormous series of volumes?

- But that's the Universal History, compiled by a Society of Men of Letters.

- And his.

- You're right; the bastard of Folly and Wisdom delivered by Truth, and the godson of Jupiter, suckled by Foolishness, is man.

All his life he was truthful and a liar, sad and cheerful, wise and foolish, good and bad, ingenious and foolish, without ever being able to entirely erase the traits he inherited from his father, his mother, his godfather, the midwife and his nurse. Lazy, ignorant and gaudy in his childhood; carefree and libertine in his youth; ambitious and devious at fifty; philosophic and gossipy at sixty; he died with his head in his nurse's little crush, swearing that he loved his godfather madly, and being the devilishly afraid to go and find him.

As I was finishing this tale, I was visited by a young German, called Linschering, who told me a rather singular fact: that among his fellow students there was one, the laughing stock of all the others for his profound ineptitude for the study of languages.

Linschering took pity on him, and set out to relieve him of the contempt that was desolating this child, by giving him some talent that would put him on a par with the rest of the class.

He applied it to geometry, and the first lesson was the most complicated proposition of the Elements, the relationship of the sphere to the cylinder.

This problem became the center of all the theorems and problems leading to its solution, which he demonstrated successively as the need arose. As a result, this student possessed all of geometry, convinced that he knew only one proposition.

In truth, I would gladly prefer this method to the ordinary one.

In it, all truths are related to a single goal, which serves as their core. This kernel is Hercules' club, and the other truths are like nails: it's a whole that nothing can break.

The ordinary method of going from first principles to the most immediate consequences leaves truths isolated and almost without any determined application.

We begin with what has to do with lines; from there, we move on to the measurement of surfaces, and then we deal with solids. These are, so to speak, three separate and distinct courses of study: the demonstration of a very complicated proposition, such as the relationship of the sphere to the cylinder, embraces and links all three.

It seems to me that the science is established more compactly and firmly in the understanding, that it frightens the disciple less, and that, perhaps, it relieves the memory.

If this is true of geometry, it would perhaps also be true of mechanics, astronomy and the other parts of mathematics, which would thus be reduced to the solution of a fairly small number of problems.

If someone had told you, at the age of fifteen, that the whole science of mathematics could be reduced to the solution of twelve problems..., I have no doubt that you would be a mathematician today.

The multitude of propositions puts us off more than the scope of a few.

SECOND VOLUME

SECTION V.

CHAPTER I.

How do we demonstrate that the moon is the cause of the ebb and flow of the sea? It is by the rigorous correspondence of the variety of the tides with the variety of the moon's movements. Now, what correspondence could be more rigorous than that between the state of my body and the state of my mind? What vicissitude, however slight, does not pass from my organization to my intellectual functions? I sleep badly, I think badly; I digest badly, I think badly; I suffer, and my mind is sluggish; I recover my strength, and my mind its vigor. The vice and quality of my mind remain or pass, depending on whether the disturbance of my organs is constant or momentary. There are even singular circumstances where the disorder of my animal economy benefits my mind, and, conversely, where the disorder of my mind benefits my body. A man does not become apoplectically overweight without his head and mind becoming weighed down. The healthy or unhealthy state of the organs, lasting or passing, for one day or for the whole course of life, from the moment of birth to the moment of death, is the thermometer of the mind.

CHAPTER II.

Page 13. - Is man good or bad at birth?

If we can only give the name of good to those who have done good, and the name of evil to those who have done evil, then surely man, at birth, is neither good nor evil. The same is true of wit and stupidity.

But does man at birth bring with him organic and natural dispositions to say and do foolish things, to harm himself and his fellows, to listen to or neglect the advice of his parents, to diligence or laziness, to justice or anger, to respect or contempt for laws? Only he who has never seen two children in his life, and never heard their cradle cries, can doubt this. Man is born with nothing, but each man is born with his own aptitude for something.

- Monsieur Helvétius, you are a hunter, I believe?

- Yes, I am a hunter.

- Do you see that little dog there?

- It's got long, low legs, a pointed muzzle, fire-spotted paws and skin?

- Yes. What is it?

- It's a basset hound; this species has a nose, ardor, courage: it'll shove itself down a foxhole, just in case, and come out with torn ears and flanks.

- And this other one?

- It's a hound. It's an indefatigable animal: its hard, bristly coat enables it to burrow into thick, thorny bushes; it stops partridges; it hunts hares by voice; it can single-handedly take the place of three or four dogs.

- And this other one?

- He'll be one of the finest sighthounds around.

- And the third?

- A sundog. I can't tell you anything about him: will he be docile or not? Will he have a nose or not? It's a question of breed.

- And the fourth?

- He promises to be a very fine hound.

- Are they all dogs?

- Yes, they are.

- And, tell me, I have an excellent gamekeeper, he'll do anything I want; couldn't I order him to make the basset hound a braque, the braque a greyhound, the greyhound a plains dog, the plains dog a hound, and the hound a barbet?

- You'd better watch out.

- And why? They're just born, they're nothing; fit for anything, education will dispose of them as I see fit.

- You've got to be kidding me.

- Monsieur Helvétius, you're right. But what if there were the same variety of individuals in the human species as in the breed of dogs, if each had its own pace and its own game?

CHAPTER III.

Page 15 - Evil from others is but a dream.

You're misinterpreting this proverb. In other words, the harm that befalls another affects me less than the same harm that befalls me.

CHAPTER IV.

Page 23. - If the stag's bark moves me, if his tears bring tears to my eyes, this spectacle, so touching in its novelty, is pleasing to the savage whom habit hardens to it.

- Why does the barking stag move you? What is the reason for your commiseration for an animal in whose place you don't put yourself?

- Novelty.

- Novelty surprises and doesn't touch. This commiseration is from animal to animal, or if we prefer, it's a quick illusion brought on by symptoms of pain common to man and animal, and which shows us a man in the place of a deer.

Page 24. - If the people return to the public executions, it is not to see suffering; on the contrary, they go to seek a feeling of pity, a subject for peroration; on his return, he plays a role, the neighbors gather around him, pendentes ab ore loquentis.

Ibid. - I would compare a battlefield to the table of a ruinous game. The victorious soldier takes the remains of the dying soldier, just as the wealthy gambler takes the purse of the desperate gambler. I use it with others as they would have used it with me; why should I have a foolish pity today that I won't find tomorrow?

Page 25 - He who commiserates with his master washes his hands in his own blood. Saadi says so.

But this poet relates that an unfortunate man dragged to the ordeal was charging the tyrant with imprecations, that the tyrant, too far away from the unfortunate man to hear him, having asked what he was saying, a courtier replied:

"Lord, he says that he who shows mercy in this world will obtain it in the next..." that another courtier taking up the word, added: Lord, you are being lied to; the wretch you have condemned to torment for his crimes would deserve it by the imprecations he spews against you... - Never mind," said the Sultan, "I will pardon him, let him go; I prefer a lie that makes me merciful to a truth that would make me cruel. "

Page 26. - There are good men, but humanity in them is the effect of education, not nature.

Always! I don't believe it. Whatever education was given to the ferocious beast who was examining with curious joy the convulsions of the Capuchin he had murdered, I find it hard to imagine that it would have made him a very tender and compassionate man.

One does not give what nature has refused; perhaps one destroys what nature has given. The cultivation of education improves his gifts.

Ibid. - Physical sensitivity is nature's only gift to us.

But is this sensitivity diffused in all parts of man equally shared between them? It is not, it cannot be.

If the portion of physical sensitivity is weak in the brain and diaphragm, there is little imagination, little pity, little benevolence.

Is physical sensitivity equal in all individuals? It is not, it cannot be.

Will you obtain the same effects from a machine in which this spring is too strong, as from one in which it is too weak?

CHAPTER V.

Page 28. - Where do we find heroes? Among more or less civilized peoples.

There are heroes everywhere: there are heroes deep in the forests of Canada whom education has not made; there are heroes in the huts of slaves whom the tyranny of their masters has not destroyed.

A troop of maroon savages is taken to Cayenne; the one who hangs his comrades is offered his life. A master orders one of his negroes to hang them all, on pain of being hanged himself. He agrees; he goes to his cabin under the pretext of preparing himself. He takes an axe, slashes his wrist, returns and says to his master, showing him his mutilated arm dripping with blood: "Now make me an executioner, if you can.

The negro's master behaved well. He grabbed his slave's bloody wrist with one hand, threw his other arm around his neck and kissed him, saying, "You're no longer my slave, you're my friend."

CHAPTER VII.

Page 37. - How, Monsieur Helvétius, you grant adolescence a greater capacity to learn than mature age, and you agree that there is hardly any other appreciable difference between these two ages than that of more or less developed organization; and you grant no effect to the organization of two children, although this organization of two children of the same age has no other difference than that of two men of different ages!

You accuse Rousseau of contradiction, and you're right; but you give him his revenge. If I ask you in several places in your first volume where the sublime thought that should illustrate such and such a man comes from, you will answer me clearly: from a lucky chance. Here, it's no longer that, it's a consequence of age, of sap, of flowers and of a fruit that knots, a chain of natural and known causes.

Page 39. - As old age approaches, man is less attached to the earth.

Is this really true?

CHAPTER VIII.

Page 41. - If character were the effect of organization, there would be a certain number of men of character in every country.

And so it is true.

Why is it that only free countries have them?

Why do we see a few in the most enslaved nations?

Is there any moral maxim that melts a magnifying glass?

Always the organization of the head compared to that of the foot. My philosopher, you will no doubt have noticed that exercise strengthens the organs, and you might have noticed that inaction destroys them. Bind one of a child's arms when he is born, make him not use it, and you will reduce that limb to nothing. In the same way, a natural disposition to some vice, virtue or talent, by dint of being thwarted, can be destroyed: the organ remains, but without vigor. For want of walking, our women have almost lost the use of their legs, but if nature had denied them legs, would there be any artificial way of giving them them? The advantage of education consists in perfecting the natural aptitude, if it is good, in stifling it or leading it astray, if it is bad, but never in making up for the aptitude that is lacking. It is to this fruitless obstinacy of ungrateful work that I would gladly attribute the swarm of imitators of all kinds. They see what others do, they strive to do what they do; their eyes are never turned inward, they are always fixed on a model outside. The kind of impulse they show is the shock of a foreign genius that communicates it to them. Nature pushes the man of genius, the man of genius pushes the imitator. There is no intermediary between nature and genius, which is always interposed between nature and the imitator. Genius strongly attracts to itself everything within its sphere of activity, exalting it beyond measure. The imitator does not attract, he is attracted; he is magnetized by contact with the magnet, but he is not the magnet.

Page 44. - Hunger is renewed several times a day, and becomes a very active principle in the savage.

This may be so, but this imperious principle produces fewer crimes in a hundred years among savages than are committed in China, in the wisest of empires, in a month of famine.

What I say about hunger is even truer of all other passions.

So you prefer the savage state to the police state? No. The population of the species always increases in the case of policed peoples, and decreases in the case of savage nations. The average lifespan of policed man exceeds the average lifespan of savage man. That says it all.

The happiest country is not the one with the fewest storms; it's the one that produces the most fruit. I'd rather live in fertile countries where the earth constantly trembles underfoot, threatens to engulf and sometimes does engulf men and their dwellings, than languish on an arid, sandy, tranquil plain. I'll be wrong when I see the people of Saint-Domingue or Martinique seeking the deserts of Africa.

Yes, Monsieur Rousseau, I prefer refined vice under a silk suit to ferocious stupidity under a beast's skin.

I like voluptuousness better between the gilded panelling and on the soft cushions of a palace, than pale, dirty, hideous misery stretched out on the damp, unhealthy earth and hidden with fear in the depths of a wild den.

CHAPTER IX.

Page 49 - Rousseau said to himself: Men, in general, are lazy, and therefore enemies of any study that forces them to pay attention. Men are vain, and therefore enemies of any superior spirit. Finally, mediocre men have a secret hatred for scholars and science. Let me persuade them of their uselessness, I will flatter the vanity of the stupid, I will make myself dear to the ignorant, I will be their master, they my disciples, and my name, consecrated by their praise, will fill the universe, etc.

Rousseau did not say all this to himself, you slander him; he is not a villain by system, he is an eloquent orator, the first dupe of his sophisms.

Whatever revolution takes place in people's minds, Rousseau will never fall into the category of despised authors. He will be among literati what bad draftsmen are among painters, great colorists.

CHAPTER X.

Page 53 - In the same chapter where I read a reproach that men of letters have deserved, that of having worshipped tyrants, I read the name of Frederick alongside that of Antonin.

Frederick angered all the poets, philosophers, orators and scholars of Germany with his contempt.

CHAPTER XI.

Page 54. - Nations are barbarous when they found empires, and it is when they return to barbarism that empires dissolve.

These two moments of barbarism are but two dates, one of origin, the other of end. If the peoples who attacked the Roman Empire from all sides had not been barbarians, its destruction would have been much more rapid. If the Romans had not fallen back into barbarism when they were attacked by the barbarians, I doubt they would have been subjugated. Here I join Helvétius against Rousseau.

Page 56 - In all kinds of commerce, demand precedes supply.

I don't think this is always true. An ingenious artist invents a luxury object, he executes it, he produces it, he pleases: at once countless demands are addressed to him, he satisfies them and is rich. It's true that the moment demand ceases, art disappears.

NOTES.

Page 61. - It's not the feeling of moral beauty that makes the worker work, but the promise of twenty-four sous for a drink.

I don't know if it's the former, but experience has often taught me that it's not always the latter. There is such an honest workman who is so jealous of his reputation that he would be offered money to do a bad job. I knew one who excelled in the art of working the surgical instruments whose operations he was familiar with; although his fortune was not considerable, and there was much more to be gained by lending himself to the visions of a bad surgeon than by making a good instrument, a large sum of money would not have determined him to do so: he would have regarded himself as an accomplice in a fatal operation; he made no difference between a workman who would have made such an instrument, against his better judgement and conscience, and one who would have made a dagger intended to kill the patient.

Page 62. - When we no longer perceive the suffering to which we ourselves are subject, we become hardened.

I do not believe that this is the reason why a doctor or surgeon becomes hardened; it is because sensitivity weakens through habit. The doctor ceases to sympathize, much as, in a long illness, the patient, and in long misfortune, the unfortunate, cease to complain, or, more exactly, as, at the fourth performance of a tragedy, the spectator ceases to weep.

Ibid. - Both the wicked and the good are susceptible to friendship.

That may be so. However, I find it hard to conceive of true friendship between villains: the villain sees in the death of his friend little more than the loss of a confidant in his crimes. Two villains must fear each other and can hardly esteem each other.

Page 63. - We see children smearing beetles and kites with hot wax, dressing them up as soldiers, and thus prolonging their death for two or three months. In vain will it be said that these children do not reflect on the pain these insects suffer. If the feeling of compassion were as natural to them as that of fear, it would alert them to the suffering of the insect, just as fear alerts them to the danger of a furious animal.

Commiseration seems to me to be no less natural than fear. One presupposes knowledge of pain, the other of peril.

Page 67. - Some officers want soldiers to be automatons.

Why is that? Is it not that discipline is more useful today than intelligence and courage? I believe that the general cares very much about being obeyed and fears very little about being judged.

SECTION VI.

CHAPTERS III TO XVIII INCLUSIVE.

Page 121. - The author has so complicated the question of luxury, that after reading everything he has to say about it, one can scarcely have clearer notions of it.

I give the name of luxury to everything that is beyond necessary needs, relative to the rank that each citizen occupies in society.

According to this definition, the history of luxury seems to me to be written in large letters above the doors of every house in the capital.

When it comes to luxury, I divide citizens into three classes: the rich, the well-off and the poor.

There is no luxury in the rich man, if he does not allow his tastes, his passions, his fantasies, to exceed the fair limits prescribed by his wealth. He has gold; what use do we expect him to make of it, except to multiply his pleasures?

There is no luxury in the well-to-do citizen, if he has no tastes, passions or ruinous fantasies.

There can be no luxury in the poor, since they lack the necessities of life.

Luxury is therefore born of a foolish use of one's fortune.

And what can be the cause of this foolish use, not just in one citizen, but in an entire nation?

The cause? It is the excessive importance attached to wealth, combined with an unequal distribution of wealth.

Society then divides into two classes: a very small class of citizens who are rich, and a very large class of citizens who are poor.

In the first class, luxury is an ostentation of wealth; in the second, luxury is a mask for misery. This ostentation, pushed to excess, leads to the ruin of the rich, and hence to the short-lived nature of great fortunes.

This mask fills the misery of the poor.

This kind of luxury is necessarily followed by the corruption of morals, the decadence of taste and the downfall of all the arts.

By foolish emulation, there are no extravagances into which the rich do not rush, no basenesses to which the poor do not commit themselves.

The exterior confounds all ranks. To support this exterior, men and women, great and small, all prostitute themselves in a hundred different ways. Poverty is the only thing to be ashamed of.

We make many statues, but we make them badly; we make many paintings, but we don't make any good ones; we make many clocks and watches, but we make them badly. Nothing is useful, everything is for show.

If we assume a more equal distribution of wealth and a national affluence proportionate to different conditions, if gold ceases to be the representation of all kinds of merit, then we will see the birth of another luxury. This luxury, which I call the good one, will produce effects quite the opposite of the first.

If the common woman wants to buy a dress, she won't ask for it to be light and flashy, because she'll have enough to pay for it to be durable, solid and well-made.

If she fancies having her hair painted, she won't call in a dauber.

If she wants a watch, it won't be enough for the flattened button to simulate a repeater.

There will be few crimes, but many vices, but of those vices that make for happiness in this world and for which one is only punished in the next.

I therefore think that a sovereign would have nothing better to do than to work with all his might for the damnation of his subjects.

All this is just a sketch, but I'm making a note and not a Treatise.

CHAPTER VI.

THE FORMATION OF PEOPLES.

Page 90 - A few families have moved to an island. I want the soil to be good, but uncultivated and deserted. When these families disembark, what is their first concern? To build huts and clear the land necessary for their subsistence. What were the island's riches? Crops and the labor that produces them...

These are assumptions I can hardly be satisfied with. In the first moment there will be no wealth, everyone will cultivate for their present needs, and the lazy man will risk starvation; for, lacking everything, what could he give in exchange for the food he has not collected? And he whose arms will have been the most active and the strongest, what will he do with the superfluity of his harvest? But let's not quibble, and move on.

Page 91 - There is only one way to remove an empire from the despotism of the army, and that is for its inhabitants to be citizens and soldiers, as in Sparta.

Wherever every citizen is a soldier, there is no need for an army. An army, no matter who leads it, threatens the freedom of other citizens. When the presence of the enemy does not require it, all inhabitants must be armed or disarmed; those who are in a body have too much advantage over those who are isolated.

CHAPTER VII.

Page 97. - On the occasion of a people governed by representatives and a monarch, such as England, I will say the idea that comes to me, perhaps true, perhaps false. It was imagined that the law forbidding the corrupting of peoples, the oath of strict compliance with this law, and consequently all freedom preserved in the appointment of representatives, would make the English nation the best governed and most formidable in the world. On this point, I thought that since representation no longer cost anything to the representative, it would be all the cheaper for the court. I replied that Walpole had the tariff of all the probity in the kingdom, and that the only effect of the proposed law would be to lower that tariff.

CHAPTER IX.

Page 102. - But there is another source of the inequality of industries and of the parsimony of fathers who must sometimes transmit immense wealth to their children. These fortunes are legitimate, and I do not see how, with justice and respect for the sacred law of property, we can obviate this cause of luxury.

Answer. It's that there's no need to obviate it; it's that fortunes will be legitimately distributed when the distribution is proportionate to the industry and work of each person; it's that this inequality will have no unfortunate consequences; on the contrary, it will be the basis of public happiness if a means is found, not to debase, but to diminish the importance of gold; and this means, the only one I know of, is to abandon all dignities and all State positions to competition.

Then an opulent father will say to his son: My son, if all you want are castles, dogs, wives, horses, delicacies and exquisite wines, you shall have them; but if your ambition is to be something in society, that's your business, not mine; work by day, work by night, educate yourself, for with all my fortune I wouldn't make you a bailiff.

Then education will take on a great character, then the child will feel all its importance; for if he asks who is the great chancellor of France, it will often happen that he will be named the son of his father's carpenter or tailor, perhaps that of his shoemaker.

If competitors are judged on their morals and enlightenment, if vices as surely lead to exclusion as ignorance, there will be honest people and skilled people.

I don't pretend that this method is without disadvantages, or that, whoever the judges of merit may be, there will be no predilection, no partisanship, no partiality of any kind; but there is a modesty that even today has sometimes imposed it on ministers, and I don't think anyone would dare prefer a rascal or a fool to an honest and enlightened competitor. The worst thing that could happen is that, perhaps, the most worthy candidate would not always be appointed to the vacant post.

Only the contest of merit for the highest positions can reduce gold to its true value.

In this supposition I ask what strange motive could determine a father to torment himself all his life in order to accumulate only goods and pass on to his son only the means to be a miser, or a dissipator or a voluptuary?

At the same time as merit will be more honored, greed diminished, the price of education better felt, fortunes will be less unequal. These desired effects are necessarily linked to one another.

The only truly desirable wealth is that which satisfies all life's needs, and which enables fathers to provide excellent teachers for their children.

All the consequences of the above principles are easy to draw.

Without good public morals, there can be no true taste; without education and probity, there can be no honors to pursue. A sovereign may shower his favorite with riches, but he can give him neither knowledge nor virtue.

CHAPTER XI

Page 105. - The means the author proposes to prevent the inequality of fortunes displease me. They hinder liberty, must harm industry and commerce, and give citizens a spirit of falsehood: they will be constantly occupied with ways to hide their wealth and dispose of it as they please.

Page 106. - The rich man supplied with the necessities of life will always put the superfluity of his money towards the purchase of superfluities.

And what does it matter if he has magots on his mantelpiece, provided there are none in our courts?

CHAPTER XII.

Page 107 - A people without money, if enlightened, is usually without a tyrant.

I believe so; but is it very easy for nations to become enlightened, without a conventional sign of all the things necessary for life? Destroy this driving principle, and you will see the birth of a state of general stagnation; and is this state very favorable to the progress of science, the arts, and the perfection of the human spirit? Just now you defended knowledge against Jean-Jacques, and now you're opening the door to universal ignorance.

CHAPTER XIII.

Page 111 - He who can give money doesn't always give it to the most honest person.

And what do I care if he makes whores, as long as whores don't make ministers?

You can certainly inflame a people with the passion of glory without the intervention of gold, that is to say, you will have very belligerent subjects, conquerors, knights, paladins; for scholars, I release you, unless your little colony placed like Lacedemona, is surrounded by educated nations: but then its duration will be very precarious.

The general resolution of all nations to throw all their gold into the sea is absurd to suppose. It is therefore far more reasonable to reduce wealth to its natural advantages, by means of an institution that requires only a pure and simple act of the sovereign's will; it would only be a question of generalizing a law that already exists in a few particular cases, where its good effects are obvious. All the chairs in our Faculty of Law are open to competition, and there is not one that is not filled by a man of merit.

CHAPTER XVI.

Page 113. - The love of money is destructive of talent, patriotism and virtue.

Yes, money representative of all merit, I grant; money representative only of voluptuousness, I deny.

Why do we want to have gold, and then what? more gold? Because gold gives you everything: consideration, power, honors, even wit.

If with gold you had only those things that could be paid for, and if you were deprived of all those things that could not be discounted, gold would be very inoffensive; benevolence, humanity and compassion would be even more common. Today, when money is everything, one is and must be stingy with an ecu; an ecu is too many things at once to be liberal with it.

I don't know whether the ministry would be equally greedy, but it could not lose its prerogatives without the nation becoming less stingy.

CHAPTER XVIII.

Page 121. - Whoever declares himself the protector of ignorance, declares himself the enemy of the State.

Now, whoever declares himself the enemy of gold, without restriction, declares himself, or I am very much mistaken, the protector of ignorance.

NOTES.

Page 127. - The monarch must be stingy with the good of his subjects.

This reminds me of a remark made by the reigning Empress of Russia. Falconet had come to Petersburg with quite a large number of paintings he had collected in England. The Empress saw them and took only a few, and at a very moderate price, adding that Falconet Sr. would be unhappy, but that he would not consider that it was not she who was paying.

Ibid. - What is the sign of harmful luxury? By the kind of merchandise displayed in the stores. The richer the merchandise, the lower the proportion of the citizen's wealth.

Instead of saying the richer these goods are, it might have been more accurate to say: the worse these goods are, the more wealth they display; the more unequal the fortunes, the more widespread the luxury of misery.

Stores where the goods are truly rich are few and far between. Those where the apparent richness of the goods serves as a mask for misery are without number.

Page 131. - Let half the wealth of a nation be wiped out, if the other half is more or less equally distributed among all the citizens, the state will be almost equally happy and powerful.

I doubt one and deny the other. How can it remain so powerful, if the surrounding and rival nations have retained all their wealth? How can it be so happy, if its pleasures are less? And they will be, thanks to everything that their modest fortunes won't allow them to bring in at great expense from distant lands.

Burgundy and Champagne wines are hardly drunk in Switzerland. Reduce the wealth of the Swiss by half, and they will drink far less.

A country needs, says Helvétius (page 132), either money, the laws of Sparta, or the danger of a forthcoming invasion. The laws of Sparta would be the ruin of the nation, if it were possible to introduce them. Helvétius says so. The greater the sum of wealth, the greater the danger of invasion. How, then, could he assure us, in the previous paragraph, that if half our gold were thrown into the sea, we would be neither less happy nor less powerful?

Ibid. - The most common crime of European governments is their greed to appropriate all the people's money.

You increase the diligence of bees by castrating them of part of their wax and honey. Take all, and the bees leave the hive; take too much, and the bees stay and die.

Page 135. - Honors are a currency that rise and fall according to the more or less justice with which they are distributed.

The debasement of honors poorly bestowed produces the same effect on morale as the alteration of currencies on the physique.

Ibid. - What is the cause of England's extreme power? To its government.

But to what cause can we attribute the poverty of Scotland and Ireland, and the extravagance of the present war against the colonies? To the greed of metropolitan merchants.

This nation is praised for its patriotism. I defy anyone to show me in ancient or modern history a more marked example of national personality or anti-patriotism.

I see this people under the emblem of a vigorous child who is born with four arms, but whose one arm tears off the other three.

Another observation that stains the character of this nation in my eyes is that its Negroes are the most unfortunate of Negroes. The Englishman, an enemy of tyranny at home, is the most ferocious despot when he is outside it.

Where does this oddity come from, if it's real as we're sure it is? Does he relieve himself far away from the empire of the law that keeps him hunched over in his homes? Or is it only the result of the contempt he has for those who have the baseness to submit to the arbitrary authority of a master?

SECTION VII.

CHAPTER I.

Page 139. - When King James said it was difficult to be both a good theologian and a good subject, he was repeating the proverb that says it is difficult to serve two masters at once.

CHAPTER IV.

Page 151. - The Jesuit doctrine favored petty theft; yet the magistrate who condemned it out of decency had not noticed that it had multiplied the number of thieves.

In fact, there are a multitude of domestic skulduggery schemes that do not come to the magistrate's attention.

A preacher of theft confined in a sort of box where he talks in my valet's ear does not seem to me to be a character at all indifferent to the safety of my person and effects.

CHAPTER V.

THE GOVERNMENT OF THE JESUITS.

A true observation, which I have not read in any author, is that one loved a Jacobin, a Capuchin, another monk, without loving the order; instead, the friend of a Jesuit was the friend of the Jesuits. The smallest part represented the whole.

Page 170 - Here the author is disjointed. There is no muse to whom a temple has not been erected; no science that has not been cultivated in some academy; no academy where some prize has not been offered for the solution of certain problems in optics, agriculture, astronomy, mechanics, etc., etc., etc. By what fatality are the moral and political sciences, the most important of all those that contribute most to national happiness, still without public schools?

This piece has no connection with either what precedes or what follows, and was not salient enough to retain at the expense of the connection of ideas. This is not the only place where this flaw is apparent. When one is familiar with the author's way of working, one must be surprised not to recognize it more often in his work.

Page 171. - I agree that monastic laws should be the most perfect; I deny that they are the most durable. Only what conforms to nature, which never ceases to claim its rights, is durable.

Neither Helvétius, nor any of the writers who preceded or followed him, fully understood the primitive nature of Jesuitism.

When they presented themselves in France and were asked what they were:

regular? They said no; secular? They said no, and they were right.

Their founder was a military man. Their institution was military: Christ was the leader of the troop, the general was its colonel; the rest were either captains, lieutenants, sergeants or soldiers.

Laughable, but no less true.

It was a true order of chivalry. And what were the enemies they had to fight? The devil, or unbelief, vice and ignorance. They went on missions near and far against unbelief. They preached in the towns against vice, they ran schools against ignorance; all marching under the banner of the Virgin Mary, the Dulcinea of St. Ignatius.

Add to this the fact that the establishment of this order was almost immediate at the time of Spanish chivalry, paladins and don-quichottism.

All that remained of the founder's spirit was fanaticism. They had so degenerated under the third generalate that one of their former writers, whose name I cannot recall, said to them: "You have become ambitious and political; you chase gold; you despise study and virtue; you associate with the great. You are moving so quickly towards vice and power, that sovereigns will desire your extinction and will not know how to carry it out."

NOTES.

Page 173. - It is true that military law compels a soldier to shoot his companion and friend; but it is an atrocious law against which people have always protested.

Is it right to blame a nation for the vice of a particular state? Is it right to reproach a civilized century for a law established in a barbaric age?

It's a way of reasoning as singular as that of a historian who would claim to prove by the example of Brutus that, in the early days of Rome, fathers either didn't love their children, or loved them less than their country. Among all the citizens, perhaps only this man was capable of his heroic or ferocious action; the general astonishment it caused proves this enough.

It would be very poor judgment of the general spirit of a people to conclude its strength or weakness, the purity or corruption of its morals, its wealth or poverty, from the actions of a few individuals, and to say: "Apicius let himself starve to death, because it was no longer possible for him to live on the eight or nine hundred thousand pounds he had left; so a Roman, then, was in misery with this capital."

Ibid. - Is there a moment when man's freedom can be related to the different operations of his soul?

This sentence is suspicious.

Page 174. - There is hardly a saint who has not once in his life washed his hands in human blood.

I have the utmost contempt for the saints, but I cannot bring myself to slander them; unless by the austerities they exercised on themselves and to which they encouraged others by their example and advice, one believes oneself authorized to regard them as suicides or assassins, and this is perhaps the author's thought.

Page 177. - Why so few honest men? It is because misfortune pursues probity almost everywhere.

There is no people so generally corrupt that a few virtuous men cannot be found among them; among these virtuous men there is perhaps not a single one who has not attained honors and wealth by the sacrifice of his virtue. I would like to know by what quirk they refused to do so, what motive they had for preferring indigent and obscure probity to opulent and decorated vice.

Ibid. - It is true that religion made Henri IV return a shield, but it made him stab himself.

Page 178. - I cannot dispense with recalling here the speech I heard made to a Sorbonne doctor, the Abbé L'Avocat, the house librarian. At the time, the Keeper of the Seals, Machault, was planning to extinguish ecclesiastical immunities. Here," said the doctor, "is a quarrel that would soon be over, if I were in the archbishop's place.

- What would you do?

- What would I do? I'd go to Madame de Pompadour and tell her: Madame, you're living in scandalous commerce with the king; I warn you that if within a week you haven't returned to your husband's house, I'll excommunicate you."

Page 181. - If the executioner can do anything to armies, says a great prince, he can do anything to cities.

A great prince, you say, Helvétius! say a great villain, a Caesar Borgia. Woe betide the nation governed by a sovereign, I do not say who leads by such principles, but whose cruel soul is capable of conceiving them.

Page 182. - The despotism of the head of the Jesuits cannot be harmful.

To his order, I agree; but to society? you don't think so.

And if the sovereign were to govern his empire according to the principles of

Jesuitical policy, how do you think other sovereigns would fare?

A nation where all its subjects were in the hands of the sovereign like a stick in the hand of an old man, where the sovereign commanded all his subjects like the Old Man of the Mountain commanded his fanatics, would incessantly exterminate all other nations, or be incessantly exterminated by them.

What murders, what assassinations I see committed! What rivers of blood I see flowing on all sides! The very idea makes me shudder. Would such a monarch be threatened by one of his neighbors with a just or unjust war? He would only have to say: "Let's go kill him..." and instantly thousands of arms would be at his command.

SECTION VIII.
CHAPTER II.

THE USE OF TIME.

Page 188. - I have read this chapter with the greatest pleasure; I do not have the strength to contradict it in form, but I do fear that there is a little more poetry than truth in it. I would have more confidence in the delights of a carpenter's day, if it were a carpenter who told me about it, and not a general farmer whose arms have never experienced the hardness of wood and the heaviness of the axe. This blessed carpenter, I see him wiping the sweat from his brow, putting his hands on his hips and relieving the fatigue of his loins with rest, panting every moment, measuring the thickness of the beam with his compass. Perhaps it's very sweet to be a carpenter or a stonemason, but frankly I don't want that kind of happiness, even with the pleasant memory, with each stroke of the axe or saw, of the payment that awaits me at the end of my day.

All kinds of work provide equal relief from boredom, but not all are equal. I don't like those that quickly lead to old age, and they are neither the least useful, nor the least common, nor the best rewarded.

The fatigue is such that the worker is much more sensitive to the cessation of his work than to the benefit of his salary: it is not his reward, it is the hardness and length of his task that occupies him throughout his day. The word that escapes him when the day's fall takes the spade from his hand is not: "I'm going to get my money..." it's: "I'm even for today.

And do you think that when he's back home, he's in a hurry to throw himself into his wife's arms? Do you think he's as eager as an idler in his mistress' arms? Almost all the children of the poor are only made on the morning of a Sunday or holiday.

I did, however, make an experiment that I'll relate: you can draw all the conclusions you want from it. I was returning from the Bois de Boulogne with a friend. This friend said to me: "We're going to meet some carriages going to Versailles; I bet we won't see a serene face in any of them...". Indeed, all of them either had their heads bent over their chests, or their bodies thrown into one of the corners of their carriages, with an air more dreamy and worried than I can paint it for you. But that's not all: several of these unfortunates, busy sawing stone along the banks of the river, were singing along, biting hungrily into a piece of brown bread. So, you say, the latter was happier than the former? Yes, in that moment, on that day perhaps. But we're not talking about a moment, or a day. The stonemason sawed stone every day and didn't sing every day. The man of the court wasn't on his way to Versailles all day, didn't go there every day, and wasn't always sad, either going there or coming back.

If the stonemason felt less pain from a very hard vein of stone than the courtier from the monarch's inadvertence or his minister's furrowed brow, a look from the monarch, a favorable word from his minister made the courtier happier than the stonemason was by a soft vein of stone that lessened his fatigue and shortened his work.

On the other hand, I don't believe that the lord who is deprived of the sovereign happiness of supping in the small apartments, is as satisfied at his table or that of his friends, despite the delicacy of the dishes and the variety of the most exquisite wines, as the stonemason, back from the port in his thatched cottage, with his jug of water or his pot of bad beer, next to his wife and children.

But if one is unhappy, it's because he has a bad head; and that religion, the habit of misery and work, along with the best judgment, are barely enough for the other to reconcile him with his state.

Finally, Helvétius, which of the two would you rather be, a courtier or a stonemason? A stonemason, you might say. However, before the day was out, you'd be fed up with the saw, which you'd have to take up again the next day; and you'd soon have sent the monarch, his minister and the whole court packing, if your role as courtier displeased you.

Believe me, eight or ten hours of sawing would soon have eased your troubles at L'Œil-de-Bœuf.

I know very well that every state has its disgraces. When I was fifteen, I read again at thirty, in Horace, that we only feel the pains of our own, and I laughed at the lawyer who envies the farmer's lot, and the farmer who envies the merchant's lot, and the merchant who envies the soldier's lot, and the soldier who swears and storms against the dangers of his trade, the modesty of his pay and the harshness of his corporal or captain ; With all this I'd rather lie nonchalantly in my armchair, my curtains drawn, my cap tucked back over my eyes, busy breaking down ideas, than beating the cement, though I make no comparison of the scolding of the piker and the satire of the envy-ridden critic full of bad faith. Certainly a whistle blow in the theater does more harm to an author than ten strokes of the stick do to the lazy or clumsy laborer; but, after eight days, the whistled author thinks no more of it, and the plaster still weighs equally on the bent shoulders of the bird-bearer.

CHAPTER III.

Page 193. - Boredom is an evil almost as dreadful as indigence.

That's what a rich man who's never had to worry about his dinner says.

I can see from the preference Helvétius gives to the condition of valet over that of master, that he has been a good master, and that he is unaware of the brutality, harshness, moodiness, weirdness and despotism of most others.

To serve is the last of the conditions, and it's never just laziness or some other vice that makes one swing between livery and hooks. Since they had strong shoulders and sinewy hocks and preferred to empty a commode than carry a burden, they were vile souls.

So it's not the large number of valets, it's the very small number of good ones that should astonish.

Ibid. - Of all the reflections on this page and the next, I will make only one, and that is that there are many states in society which exceed fatigue, which quickly exhaust strength and shorten life, and whatever wages you attach to work, you will not prevent either the frequency or the justice of the worker's complaint.

Have you ever thought of how many unfortunate people the exploitation of mines, the preparation of ceruse lime, the transport of driftwood, the cleaning of pits cause appalling infirmities and death?

Only the horrors of misery and stupefaction can reduce man to these tasks. Ah, Jean-Jacques, you've made a poor case for the savage state versus the social state!

Yes, the rich man's appetite is no different from the poor man's, and I even believe that the poor man's appetite is much livelier and truer; but for the health and happiness of both, perhaps we should put the poor man on the rich man's diet, and the rich man on the poor man's diet. It's the idle man who gorges himself on succulent foods, it's the toiling man who drinks water and eats bread, and both perish before the term prescribed by nature, one from indigestion and the other from starvation. It is the one who does nothing who drinks long draughts of the generous wine that would repair the strength of the one who works.

If the poor and the rich were equally hard-working and frugal, not everything would be compensated between them. The difference in food and work, poor and succulent food, moderate and continuous food, would still make a big difference between the average length of their lives.

Either do without metals, or allow the mines to be pestilential.

The mines of the Hartz harbor in their immense depths thousands of men who barely know sunlight and rarely reach the age of thirty. This is where we see women who have had twelve husbands.

If you close these vast tombs, you ruin the state and condemn all Saxon subjects either to starvation or expatriation.

How many workshops there are in France itself, less numerous but almost as fatal!

When I review the multitude and variety of causes of depopulation, I am always astonished that the number of births exceeds the number of deaths by one nineteenth.

If Rousseau, instead of preaching that we should return to the forest, had been busy imagining a kind of society that was half-police and half-wild, we would, I think, have had a hard time answering him.

Man has come together to fight with the greatest advantage against his constant enemy, nature; but he has not been content to defeat her, he has sought to triumph over her. He found the hut more convenient than the cave, and lodged himself in a hut; all very well, but what an enormous distance from the hut to the palace! I doubt it. How much trouble he has gone to in order to add only superfluities to his lot and complicate the work of his happiness to infinity!

Helvétius rightly said that the happiness of an opulent man was a machine in which there was always something to remake. This seems to me to be much truer of our societies. I don't agree with Rousseau that we should destroy them when we could, but I am convinced that man's industry has gone much too far, and that if it had stopped much sooner and it had been possible to simplify its work, we'd be no worse off. The Chevalier de Chastellux has distinguished very well between a brilliant reign and a happy one; it would be just as easy to assign the difference between a brilliant society and a happy one. Helvétius placed the happiness of social man in mediocrity; and I believe that there is similarly a term in civilization, a term more in keeping with the happiness of man in general and much less distant from the savage condition than we imagine; but how can we return to it when we have strayed from it, how can we remain there when we are there? I don't know. Alas, the social state may have moved towards that fatal perfection we enjoy, almost as necessarily as white hairs crown us in old age. Ancient legislators only knew the savage state. A modern legislator, more enlightened than them, who founded a colony in some unknown corner of the earth, would perhaps find between the savage state and our marvellous civilized state a milieu which would retard the progress of Prometheus' child, which would protect him from the vulture, and which would fix civilized man between the savage's childhood and our decrepitude.

CHAPTER IV.

Page 195. - The idea of virtue and the idea of happiness will become disunited in time, but this will be the work of time, and even of a long time.

It seems to me that Helvétius says elsewhere that this dissociation of ideas will be the work of an instant, that the tyrant has only to speak, and that it will be done.

Ibid. - But with better laws established, do we imagine that without being equally rich or powerful, men will believe themselves equally happy?

Does not experience of the pains of our state and ignorance of the pains of the state of others begin to separate the idea of happiness from our mediocrity of fortune, and attach it to the idea of the power and wealth of which we are deprived? If so, your good laws will have served little purpose.

No, certainly, the idea of happiness is not associated with the idea of gold and dignities in the depths of forests where there are neither dignities nor gold. But is it so at the center of a society where the child and the common man constantly see these ghosts of happiness around them, on their doorstep, beside them?

Have all our praises of the humble state, the well-to-do state, persuaded a single citizen that it was that of happiness, and extinguished in his heart the greed for gold, the ambition for honors?

CHAPTER V.

Page 198 - Wherever citizens have no share in government, where all emulation is extinguished, whoever is above need is without motive to study and to learn.

The author lived in a region such as this, he was above need, or he learned without motive, or there are still motives for learning.

Ibid. - Too lazy to anticipate pleasure, he would like pleasure to anticipate him.

Examples of such lazy people are not common. The author applies to a large class of men what is suitable only for an apoplectic and stupid Frenchman. The others seem to me to pursue amusement and pleasure with the same fury as they flee boredom. Do they always reach it? That's not the point.

Ibid. - The only way to escape boredom is with horses, dogs, carriages, concerts, musicians, painters, statues, parties and shows.

Well, you have all that, and you ruin yourself.

Either I don't know men very well, or all this (page 199) seems outrageous to me. I've often heard of unfortunate people killing themselves, but I've never heard of rich people ending their boredom in such a safe and short way.

CHAPTERS VII AND VIII.

Page 200 - It is not always habit that robs the dawn of a fine day of its freshness, the sunrise of its brilliance, the crowing of the cock, the murmur of the waters, the bleating of the herd of their pleasant sensations; it is that the soul of the possessor of these goods is sick; it is that, worked by a thousand mad passions, he arrives in his countryside like Milton's devil in the Garden of Eden. Find, if you can, the hellebore that purges his deranged brain, and you will restore to the spectacle of nature charms of which he will never tire. Everyone, tired of the frivolous amusements of the city, cries out with Horace: O rus! quando te aspiciam? ô ma terre! ô mes champs! ô mon parc! quand te reverrai-i-je? tous les revoient et tous y périssent d'ennui. You will tell me that not everyone knows how to occupy themselves there like Horace, and your reply will show me that you know nothing more about Horace's morals than you do about the human heart. The poet left Rome, convinced that it was either in his rustic hearth, or under the lime tree that shaded his fountain, that the muse and his genius awaited him; in his trunk were piled Menander on Aristophanes and this one on Plato; at his departure he had announced to his friends not one, but several masterpieces: he arrived, he enjoyed the rest and innocence of the fields. When Maecenas called him back to the city, he was furious with his benefactor, indignant that he thought his freedom had been bought with riches, and offered to return them if such a high price had been paid. The season passed, and he reappeared among his friends without having opened a book, without having written a line. Perhaps a habitual sojourn in the countryside would have made the poet forget the art of verse, without a moment's boredom. Yet who was more sought after by the great, who was more corrupted by their favors than this poet? There are souls in whom something wild remains, a taste for the idleness, frankness and independence of primitive life. They always feel alienated in cities, and carry with them a secret disgust that ceases at intervals, but soon revives, and sometimes revives in the midst of the most violent and pleasurable distractions. If he's a poet, he attributes his discomfort to importunities that prevent him from giving his all to his talent. What does he do? He wanders through the fields, stretches out nonchalantly on the meadow grass; he spends whole hours watching a brook flow; he stops by the farmer who is ploughing and talks with him about rustic work; he sometimes sits at his valets' table, enjoys their conversation, asks the barnyard lady about her geese, her pigeons, her ducks ; he orders his gardener to loosen a plot of land that seems exhausted; he sometimes digs the foot of a languishing tree himself; he plans a pump to raise the waters of his well and relieve his gardener's wife of the fatigue of pulling it; he visits his parish priest and hardly ever leaves without asking about the poor of the parish. He does everything except the thing he came to do.

CHAPTER IX.

Page 205. - I met Lady *** on a journey, who spent half the year in Paris and the rest in London, and who was equally fluent in the languages of both nations. I asked her if the morals of the French seemed to her more or less corrupt than those of the English; she replied that the only difference she found was that the vice of her compatriots seemed coarser. She added that it was the bad company of women that lost us, and that on the contrary, in her homeland the dangerous company for a man was the bad company of men.

Page 206. - Women are therefore asked to lend themselves with consideration to a minister's sad situation, and to be less difficult for him. Perhaps there is nothing to reproach them for in this respect.

If this is not in bad taste, we will at least agree that these gaieties contrast a little with the seriousness of the work.

CHAPTER X.

I would willingly treat the whole of the following chapter with the same severity. When I read the frontispiece and when I read at the top of the page about Man and his education, I am a little surprised to read, chapter X: Which mistress suits the idle man; I no longer know whether the author is an apostle of good or bad morals. I think his tone would have been less licentious if he had foreseen the advantage his enemies would take against him. There is more than one place in his book where one can be scandalized without being a bigot. When attacking religious prejudices, one cannot have or show too much restraint.

Page 207. - We need coquettes for the idle and pretty girls for the busy. Women's hunting, like that of game, must differ according to the time one wishes to put into it. Is it only possible to give it an hour or two? We go for the shot...

The skilful woman is chased for a long time by the idle man...

A woman is a well-served table that is seen in a different light before or after the meal.

Fi, fi, cross out all that big talk. We'd hardly allow ourselves to do it at the end of a dinner party, even if there weren't any women there.

The same goes for page 208.

Page 209. - Leave all those niceties to our insipid little back-alley poets; they don't sit well in the mouth of a moralist.

The desire to please everyone has made this author say many frivolous things.

CHAPTER XII.

Page 210 - When our women reach a certain age, do they leave the red, the lovers, the shows? they become devotees.

It seems to me that this custom is beginning to fall away, and that our women are neither so frequent nor so quick to take the sad step of devotion. They stay in the world, they indulge in youthful amusements; they play, they chat and chat well, because they speak from experience; they go to the country, to walks, to shows; they slander little. Their main occupation is their health, and the study of all the little comforts of life. They keep red in the face, and instead of mourning their past silliness at the feet of a priest, they laugh about it with a few close friends. This resolution, if it is real, is the result of a general contempt for religion: they stopped believing in it when they were young, and they can no longer look to it for consolation in old age. In the past, people went to mass when they left their lover's arms; today, they either don't go to mass at all, or, if they do, it's out of consideration for their servants, a constraint from which they are becoming increasingly free. Disbelief is as common among women as it is among men, a little less reasoned, but almost as firm.

CHAPTER XIII.

Page 213. - Beauty ceases to be beautiful to me in the long run.

I don't believe that. What is true remains true, what is good does not cease to be so, beauty is always beautiful. It's only my sensation that varies. I walk past the colonnade of the Louvre without looking at it, is it any less beautiful for me? By no means.

CHAPTER XIV.

Page 220 - Helvétius assumes here with Longin and Boileau a beauty in Homer that is not there. Homer does not say:

Great God, drive away the night that covers our eyes

And fight against us in the light of heaven...

He says: Great God, drive away the night that covers our eyes, and if you have resolved to lose us, at least lose us in the light of the heavens.

This passage became, some twenty years ago and more, the subject of a rather lively discussion between the Jesuit Berthier and myself. I argued that the Ajax of Longin and Boileau was a godless man, and that Homer's Ajax was pious and touching. What almost always happens to those who don't possess themselves enough is that I lost part of my advantage.

I'd like to know what the Journalist would have said to me if I'd said: Well, Father, Ajax, in your opinion, is a godless man, a sublime godless man who defies the master of the gods? However, if in the whole of the Iliad, if among all the Greek heroes, there were just one who, on the verge of engaging in a perilous battle, invited the army to pray, what would you think of this hero? would you call him an impious? would this be the character the poet intended to give him? I'm sure you know all the names of Greek chieftains by heart, but what would you call this one? Is it Achilles, Agamemnon, Patroclus, Diomedes, Ajax? Surely it can't be the latter; it would be too absurd for one who proudly addresses Jupiter and says: "Take your thunderbolt and fight against us... to say to the army: "I'm going to fight; my friends, bow down before the gods and pray for me... The soldier who would do the same today would show more religion than bravery. Yet this is Ajax himself, so consistent in Homer with his role. At the foot of Mount Ida, this is how he speaks.

> Ἀλλ' ἄγετ', ὄφρ' ἄν ἐγὼ πολεμήια τεύχεα δύω,
> Τόφρ' ὑμεῖς εὔχεσθε Διὶ Κρονίωνι ἄνακτι,
> Σιγῇ ἐφ' ὑμείων, ἵνα μὴ Τρῶές γε πύθωνται,
> Ἠὲ καὶ ἀμφαδίην, ἐπεὶ οὔτινα δείδιμεν ἔμτης-
> HOMÈRE, Iliad, Canto VII, v. 193 ff.

"Come, my friends, while I put on my breastplate, address the master of the gods; pray to him in a low voice so that the Trojans cannot hear you, or rather make your prayer aloud, for we fear no one."

Either you've misheard the poet, or the poet has misrepresented the character of his hero. Take your pick. The fault lies not with Homer, but with the commentators. But we must not confuse the error of a man of genius, such as Longin or Boileau, with the impertinence of his echo.

CHAPTER XV.

Page 223. - When a mistress is not new, it is pleasant to be at the rendezvous she has given and not to find her there.

This comment by President Hénault is that of a man who has never loved anything but pretty peccadilloes.

CHAPTER XVII.

Page 220 - It seems to me that the author does not attach enough importance to several rare qualities without which, however, one can never write well: purity of language, choice of proper or figurative expression, its place and harmony. A peasant, a man of the people will have strong ideas, striking images, but he will lack the preceding qualities which we do not get from nature, but which taste alone can give. The art of writing can be learned, but the art of thinking and feeling can hardly be taught.

CHAPTER XX.

Page 239. - It only takes a moment to admire, it takes a century to do admirable things.

Yes, to admire without judgment; but there are pieces of sculpture that have stopped me for hours on end; I have never grown weary, I will never tire of the Laocoon, I will always suffer while looking at it, and I will always tear myself away from it with difficulty. I have read and reread Homer twenty times; there are pages of Buffon whose perfection I have perhaps not yet felt; my Horace is worn and my Racine is dirty.

CHAPTER XXI.

Page 240. - I do not think that the enjoyment of a beautiful woman is like the painting of that woman and the voluptuous description of the pleasures found on her breast: the enjoyment is more vivid, the image lasts longer. An amateur is more faithful to his painting than to his mistress. A man is quicker to fall in love with objects of the senses than a man of good taste with imitations of art.

I'd rather change my troubles like a rich man than suffer the same pain over and over like a day laborer. I'd rather run after happiness, even if unsuccessfully, than stand by misfortune and misery.

Bonnier died of boredom in the midst of delight.

I don't believe it. Bonnier was bored and died of illness.

CHAPTER XXII.

Page 242 - If happiness were always the companion of power, what man would have been happier than the Caliph Abdulraman! Yet such was the inscription he had engraved on his tomb: "Honors, riches, sovereign power, I enjoyed it all. Esteemed and feared by the princes of my contemporaries, they envied my happiness, they were jealous of my glory, they sought my friendship. I have, in the course of my life, exactly marked every day on which I have tasted pure and true pleasure, and in a reign of fifty years I have counted only fourteen..."

The Caliph had calculated his days like all those who complain about life, by the great pleasures which are rare enough and by the great pains which are a little less so. If Turenne had counted only as many happy moments as he could count battles won, Turenne could have said, like the Caliph: I have only had fourteen beautiful days.

Ibid. - It is said that one is well fed and well bedded at the Bastille, and that one dies of grief there. But why? It's because you don't go about your ordinary business.

That's not it. It's that you're not in control of whether you go or don't go; it's that wherever you are, you're in a bad place, if only for a day, when you can't get out. The moment a despot says to you: I want you to stay here... he takes you back to the wild and primitive character, and if the word is stopped, the heart replies softly: I don't want to stay. And then, wouldn't you say that you have everything that makes a sensitive, honest, compassionate, studious, active man happy, when you're well fed and well bedded? The author doesn't know that anyone held in prison by the authorities, whether innocent or guilty, fears for his life, and that only the freedom he will be granted can relieve him of this terrible anxiety; he doesn't know what it is to think of a detention that will have no end, and there isn't a single unfortunate person locked up in the Bastille who doesn't have this idea.

Page 243. - The condition of the worker who, through moderate work, provides for himself and his family, is perhaps the happiest of all conditions.

Any condition that does not allow man to fall ill without falling into misery is bad.

Any condition that doesn't provide a resource in old age is bad.

If the little people lose the appalling prospect of the hospital, or if they see it without being disturbed by it, they are morons.

Everything the author says in praise of mediocrity will be contradicted by all those who feel its discomfort.

NOTES.

Page 252 - Here the author argues the case for divorce, but somewhat superficially.

He has not considered that, after divorce, children can scarcely remain either next to the father or next to the mother without being unhappy.

Here, death executes the divorce. If the survivor goes on to marry again, what happens to the children of the first marriage, mingled with the children of the second marriage, under a stepfather or stepmother? We know.

Divorce, which gives two spouses the freedom to remarry, requires that the children be taken away from them. It therefore requires guardians.

Who will you entrust with the guardianship of the children?

Nothing is so difficult as finding good guardians. The magistrate is the father of all.

To make divorce the price of merit is absurd. Is not the fool as unhappy with a bad woman as the man of the greatest genius? Doesn't enjoyment bring disgust to everyone equally? Are not all marriages indiscriminately exposed to the incompatibilities of character that are the torment of two spouses?

SECTION IX.

CHAPTER II.

Page 263. - When a family shrinks, why should it not cede part of its property to neighboring and larger families?

Why? Because this forced cession of the fruit of my industry violates the right of ownership. It wipes out all industry. Ask fathers what the object of their labors is; they'll tell you, the happiness of their children.

CHAPTER III.

Page 271. - Nothing less envied than the talent of a Voltaire or a Turenne. Proof of how little it is valued.

Proof of the difficulty of attaining it. What man is vain enough to secretly say to himself: Work, and by working you'll be Voltaire or Turenne. All you have to do is want to.

It's quite the opposite that we say to ourselves; and it only takes the recollection of a very beautiful page, ancient or modern, to knock the pen out of our hands.

CHAPTER IV.

All individual wills are ambulatory, but the general will is permanent. This is the cause of the duration of laws, good or bad, and of the vicissitude of tastes.

Page 274. - Harmful laws are sooner or later abolished.

An enlightened man is born who speaks, and his voice is heard, if not by his contemporaries, at least by his nephews.

They are not always abolished, but little by little they fall into disuse. Such is the law of adultery, and this disuse is the natural effect of their vice.

Page 275 - I am not blaming Lycurgus' laws; I merely believe them incompatible with a large state and with a trading state.

CHAPTER V.

Page 284. - The love we have for virtue in despotic countries is always false.

I don't believe it. Less common and more perilous, it must be more admired there.

CHAPTER VI.

Page 284. - The legislator who makes laws assumes all men to be wicked.

I do not believe this. If the wicked wore a visible mark on their foreheads to distinguish them, the legislator would no longer address his laws to anyone but the stigmatized. He knows there are villains, but there is no way of distinguishing them: he makes his laws general.

Page 285 - One appears to sacrifice, but one never sacrifices one's own happiness for that of others.

And what does this Curtius do when he throws himself into an abyss?

CHAPTER XVIII

Page 320 - The morals and actions of animals prove that they compare, that they make judgments; in this respect, they are more or less reasonable, more or less like man.

After this admission, I fail to see how Helvetius gives so much to organization in the comparison of man to animal, and how he can reduce its influence to nothing in the comparison of man to man.

Page 321. - The reasoning by which I have destroyed the prejudice of revenants, in order to operate its effect, must present itself as usually and as quickly as the prejudice itself.

And when it did, you would still tremble. Does thought have any power over inner movement? The tic is caught. Your head says: there are no revenants; no, there are no revenants; and your heart is troubled, and your insides are stirred, and shivering spreads through all your limbs, you are afraid. Hobbes laughs at himself, his fright makes him pity himself; and his fright lasts.

CHAPTER XIX.

Page 322 - So it is only the retention or loss of birth certificates that distinguishes the noble from the commoner?

Who would deny the title of gentleman to one who, by birth, circumcision or baptismal certificates, could prove descent in direct line from Abraham to him?

Whoever had a precise notion of nobility. Nobility does not begin until the title is granted by the sovereign; it is either the reward for a service or the mark of his favor. The distinction between nobles and commoners is a new one. The commoner Adam gave birth to the first commoner. The patriarch Abraham was a commoner, Jesus Christ was a commoner. I believe that the opposite of gentil is serf, and that the first serf who deserved by some great deed, not to be freed, but to be considered equal to his lord; the first soldier who was elevated to the rank of his chief was the first gentilhomme. The nobility is neither older nor newer than feudal government. In Athens, there were slaves and citizens; in Rome, slaves, freedmen, citizens or plebeians and patricians; in the free Gauls, chiefs and soldiers; in the Gauls, after the destruction of the Roman Empire and their division between barbarian chiefs, serfs, freedmen, lords or gentlemen, and a chief or sovereign. Incidentally, I am stating my ideas without guaranteeing their accuracy. The authors who have written on the subject of nobility should be consulted, which I would certainly do if I intended to publish these notes.

CHAPTER XX.

Page 324. - Interest makes a protector honor vice.

Witness Helvétius. He goes to Denis's court; Denis showers him with favors, and from that moment on he will only call Denis the great Prince, Prince κατ' ἐξοχὴν.

He made the journey from London. The honest way in which he treated all foreigners in France and his personal merit won him the most distinguished welcome from men of letters and the great; and the English nation became in his eyes the first of nations.

But if interest honors vice in a protector, resentment decries merit in a persecutor.

Witness Helvétius. Instead of receiving the honor and praise he was entitled to, he was exposed to a long series of disgraces that withered his heart and embittered his mood. Immediately, he saw his homeland as nothing but the meanest and vilest of nations.

However, he praised Catherine II, whom he had never met, and whose benefits did not seduce his judgment; but he was good enough to appropriate the marks of kindness I had received from her, and to make it a personal duty of gratitude. Helvétius loved his fellow students dearly. He was not an easy genius, but he was a beautiful genius, a great thinker and a very honest man.

Page 325. - Interest lights the sovereign on merit; peril and need past, he no longer distinguishes it.

I am not afraid of being accused of flattering sovereigns; but Turenne, buried at Saint-Denis and honored by the sovereign in his ashes; the victor over the Turks in the last war, Romanzoff, showered with glory and riches by the Empress of Russia, and so many others raise their voices against Helvétius' reproach.

What I would more readily accuse them of is not ingratitude, but the fact that they have often given vice and baseness the same reward as heroism and virtue, and confused the rare man with the rascal.

Recognized merit is never degraded; Catinat is forgotten, but not degraded.

Truth is persecuted, but not despised; it is feared.

What can it do for humanity? Everything in time. I don't know how it happens, but it ends up and will end up eternally stronger. Rare men to whom nature has bestowed genius and courage, your lot is assured: a long memory, blessings that will never end. Envious men, ignorant men, hypocritical men, ferocious men, cowardly men, yours is too: the execration of the centuries awaits you, and your names will either be forgotten or never uttered without the epithets I give you here.

CHAPTER XXI.

Page 326. - The interest of the powerful commands general opinion more imperiously than truth.

I don't believe it; my friends, don't believe it. If you did, you would be fools to sacrifice your rest, your health, your life to a fruitless search.

The interests of the powerful pass, the empire of truth lasts forever: the seas must cover the surface of the globe; it must be devoured by some general explosion; it must remain, this truth, or all perish with it.

Helvétius is right for a moment, but he will be wrong in the centuries to come, for which you are working.

He will appear, he will appear one day, because time brings everything that is possible, and it is possible, the just, enlightened and powerful man you are waiting for.

These truths buried in the works of the Gordons, the Syedys, the Machiavellians, are coming out on all sides, and they were only writing a moment ago.

But why shouldn't the impulse of goodness, of justice, of humanity, the fruits of a happy nature or of a good institution, precede, concur, follow the law of necessity? Why discourage nations, why distress philosophers by restricting the number of causes of happiness?

Ibid. - In the long run, it's the powerful who rule opinion.

Is this really true? A powerful man will behave as if property rights were nothing, but will he ever make us believe it? He who says to the lion: Lord, in devouring them you do them much honor, will also be a scoundrel, but will be no more credulous than the fox in the fable. The distributor of honors, riches and punishments attaches himself to people and wins applause, but he does not even enslave the souls he has corrupted. If you believe that one honors oneself with the title of slave, that one sincerely despises the state of a free man, you are referring to the grimaces of an unfortunate whose one word would break the thread that holds the sword suspended over his head.

I can think of nothing more contradictory to your principles than what you're saying here. Is the favored slave not constantly in the throes of peril? Is the oppressed slave not always in pain? How can it be that the man who fears and the man who suffers have true contempt for the man who neither fears nor suffers? You have mistaken inaction, silence or hypocrisy for the true expression of sentiment, which sooner or later, tired of its constraint, escapes with a stab that makes the tyrant's black blood run.

If the monster could command opinion, he'd be safe. And what do the religious opinions you object to prove? It's a question of man, and you speak to me of God, of a fantastic being, master of the just and the unjust, whose judgments I adore and whom I thank for the lashes with which he tears me, because they are the pledge of his commiseration for me and almost the assurance of eternal bliss.

The tyrant is a man I hate in my heart; God is a tyrant to whom I give credit for my patience, and I resign myself.

Page 327 - Without strength, what can common sense do?

Everything with time. An error falls and gives way to an error that falls again; but a truth that is born and a truth that succeeds it are two truths that remain.

CHAPTER XXIII.

Page 329 - Interest is a career of fine and great ideas.

Yes, taking the word interest in its most general sense.

CHAPTER XXIV.

Page 330 - Interest conceals from the honest priest the atrocity of his principles.

Proof that to be an honest man you need more than you think.

The priest I fear the most is not the one whose interest veils the cruelty of his principles; it's the one who doesn't impose them on himself, and whose actions are consistent with principles dictated by his avowed interest.

Religion prevents men from seeing, because it forbids them, under eternal penalty, to look.

If there is a hell in the other world, the damned see God in it, just as slaves see their master in this one. If they could kill him, they would.

CHAPTER XXX.

Page 34S. - I don't like this frivolous distinction between the religion of Jesus Christ and the religion of the priest. In fact, they are the same, and there is not a priest who would not agree.

Page 349. - Tolerance subjects the priest to the prince; intolerance subjects the prince to the priest.

So there is not a priest who does not say that tolerance or indifference in religion is the same thing under two different names; and I believe there are hardly any philosophers who deny this.

NOTES.

Page 357. - Almost all theological disputes cease when they give no preference to the dignities of the Church. If, when someone said to the monarch: "Sire, he is a Jansenist; Sire, he is a Molinist," the monarch would reply: "But does he have morals? Is he enlightened? I give him this abbey; there's nothing to stop me appointing him to this vacant episcopate..." it's not the public, it's the theologian himself who would throw scorn on the object of the dispute; it would only be mentioned in the insignificant theses of the bachelor.

Page 358. - If Poniatowski had imitated Trajan, he would have filled himself with glory throughout Europe; he would have been the idol of his country, and his generous conduct would have strangely disconcerted Poland's co-sharing powers. He would have had to assemble a Diet, take the scepter and crown, lay them down and say: "If you know one more worthy than I to reign over you, name him...". Either he would have obtained the unanimous consent of the nation to abdicate his authority, or he would have left it to another to save the country from the peril that threatened it.

SECTION X.

CHAPTER II.

THE EDUCATION OF PRINCES.

Page 377. - I find here a passage quoted from Lucian, of which there is not the first word in that author; but from Lucian, or from another, or even from me, I do not esteem it any less.

Jupiter sits at table, joking with his wife, speaking equivocal words to Venus, gazing tenderly at Hebe, slapping Ganymede on the buttocks and having his cup filled. As he drinks, he hears cries rising up from different parts of the earth: the cries redouble, he is bothered by them. He rises impatiently; he opens the trapdoor of the celestial vault and says: "Plague in Asia, war in Europe, famine in Africa, hail here, a storm elsewhere, a volcano..." then he closes his trapdoor again, goes back to the table, gets drunk, lies down, falls asleep, and calls it ruling the world.

One of Jupiter's representatives on earth gets up, prepares his own chocolate and coffee, signs orders without having read them, orders a hunt, returns from the forest, undresses, sits down to table, gets drunk like Jupiter, or like a portmanteau, falls asleep on the same pillow as his mistress, and he calls this governing his empire.

CHAPTER III.

Page 380. - Emulation is one of the chief advantages of public education over domestic.

I spent the first years of my life in public schools, and I saw four or five pupils superior to all the others succeed one another for the whole year in the places of honor, and discourage the rest of the class.

I have seen all the teacher's care concentrated in this small number of elite subjects, and all the other children neglected.

I have seen these five or six marvellous subjects occupied, for six or seven years, with the study of ancient languages they have not learned.

I've seen them all leave school stupid, ignorant and corrupt.

I have seen them pass successively under six teachers, each of whom had his own way of teaching.

I saw the students' general education neglected, to prepare two or three of them for public acts.

I saw this rule, inflexible for the children of the poor, lent itself to every little whim of the children of the rich.

I've seen the children of the rich go to their father's house twice a week to find disgust in their studies and spread it among their classmates.

And I exclaimed: Woe betide the father who can raise his child next door to him and sends him to a public school.

What's left in the world of this college institution? Nothing. The knowledge that distinguishes some college-educated men in letters, where did they get it? To their individual studies. How often have they regretted, in their study, the time they lost on the benches of a school!

So what to do? Change, from beginning to end, the method of public education.

What's next? Then, when you're rich, raise your child at home.

The education of the Greeks and Romans took place in the home, and that education was worth every penny.

It would be singular if all the care of a teacher, concentrated on one child, benefited him less than the same care shared between that child and a hundred others.

I only approve of a convent for girls when their mothers are dishonest.

I only approve of college for boys when fathers give a thousand écus to a good coachman, two thousand écus to a good cook, and want a man of merit for five hundred francs.

CHAPTER IV.

Page 383. - Physical education is neglected among almost all European peoples.

Physical education is not neglected in Petersburg. The spectacle is frightening; and the idea given in the work entitled Plans et Règlements des différents établissements de Sa Majesté impériale , etc., is accurate.

CHAPTER VI.

Page 337. - I want to make my son a Tartini.

I approve of your plan. But does your son have an ear? does he have sensitivity? does he have imagination? If he lacks these qualities, which all the masters in the world will not give him, make him whatever you please, but not a Tartini. A thousand, two thousand violins have spent days and nights with their fingers on the strings of their instrument, and have not become a Tartini; a thousand, two thousand have had the pencil in their hand from childhood, and there is still only one Raphaël. It's quite extraordinary that so far there has only been this chance. My dear philosopher, here is your madness again.

Page 389. - There are no public schools where the science of morality is taught.

The same man of judgement, M. Rivard, who introduced the study of mathematics into our public schools and substituted questions for argumentation, had proposed to teach, in place of bad scholastic morality, good elements of public and civil law. The plan was about to be implemented, when the Faculty of Law intervened, claiming that its district was being encroached upon. What happened? That public law and the law of nations were taught neither in our colleges, nor on the benches of the Faculty.

CHAPTER IX.

Page 405. - If my son learns from worldly usage that the principles I gave him in youth close the way to honors and wealth, it is a hundred to one that he will see in me only an absurd rambler, an austere fanatic, that he will despise my person, that his contempt for me will reflect on my maxims, and that he will give himself up to all the vices authorized by the form of government and the mores of his compatriots.

In verse I would pass on these exaggerations, in prose I could not. When a well-bred child realizes that his father's precepts are incompatible with the usual means of attaining honors and acquiring wealth, he finds himself at first, like Hercules at the corner of the forest, uncertain as to the path he will follow. Little by little, the general corruption overtakes him, he forgets the virtuous lessons he has received, he abandons himself to the torrent; he knows good, he approves it, he does evil. But in the midst of disorder, he respects his father, who is always for him not an absurd rambler, but a good man, whom he does not have the strength to imitate: he never comes to despise him or his principles. He never applauds himself for his vices, but excuses himself by saying that he must howl with the wolves. However, the path through the career of depravity is more or less rapid, depending on circumstances and character.

Page 407. - The praise of magnanimous men is in the mouths of all and in the hearts of none.

I believe it is in everyone's mouth and heart, because nothing is more common than the practice of vice after the most sincere praise of virtue.

Ibid. - Under despotism, a father's advice to his son is reduced to this frightening phrase: My son, be low, crawling, without virtues, without vices, without talent, without character; be what the Court wants you to be, and every moment of life remember that you are a slave.

Wherever in the world, under whatever government, I don't think a father has ever made his son hear anything like this. He will recommend circumspection, but not baseness. If he had a teacher to give him, I don't know whether he would entrust his education to a courageously virtuous man; but I'm quite sure that if he turned to his most intimate friend, he wouldn't say to him: "Wouldn't you know some witty man, well-versed in the ways of the courts, who could inspire the true maxims in my son and make him quite false, quite vile, quite hypocritical - in a word, everything you know you have to be to make your way?"

I don't know if the Maillebois has children, but if he does, I'll wager it's a good man who's bringing them up; I'll wager that if he heard this man speak to them the language you claim a father speaks to his son, he wouldn't spare him the epithets of wretch, beggar and villain, and he wouldn't suffer him for a quarter of an hour in his hotel. I bet that if this schoolmaster had inspired them with patriotism, frugality and male probity, he would never have the imprudence to say to him: "I hoped that my sons would become adroit courtiers alongside me, and you have only made heroes and virtuous men of them."

CHAPTER X.

Page 409. - A few illustrious men have shed great light on education, and yet it has remained the same.

This was neither the effect of the wickedness nor the pusillanimity of those who could and should have reinstated it, when our bad teachers were expelled; it was a consequence of their imbecility. They regarded the ideas of the reformers as chimeras, and lent themselves to an old routine which they considered the best. Let's try not to see men as more hideous than they are. The stupid believe that everything is fine as it is.

Page 410. - Here the philosopher Helvetius makes the same exhortation to courageous and enlightened men that I have made elsewhere.

SUMMARY.

SECTION II.

Page 420 - To compare is to see alternately.

Is it not rather to see together?

CHAPTER I.

THE ANALOGY OF THE AUTHOR'S OPINIONS WITH THOSE OF LOCKE.

Page 43S. - The mind is but the assembly of our ideas; ideas come through the senses; therefore the mind is but an acquisition.

Yes, an acquisition that not everyone is in a position to make.

Ibid. - To attribute it to organization, without being able to name its organ, is to recall occult qualities.

That may be so. But we name it, it's the head.

Ibid. - Experience and history teach us that the mind is independent of the greater or lesser finesse of the senses.

I don't know how far this is true.

Ibid. - Men of different constitutions are susceptible to the same passions.

This is false on all sides. We don't give ourselves all the passions. One is born angry, one is born insensitive, one is born brutal, one is born tender, and circumstances excite these passions in man, and when they would be common to all men they would not have them to the same degree.

Education does much, but it cannot do everything. Have ten children to make discreet and prudent; they will certainly all be less indiscreet and less imprudent than if no effort had been made to cultivate this virtue in them, but there will perhaps be one or two on whom education will do nothing or very little.

Page 439 - If the spirit, character and passions of men depended on the unequal perfection of their organs, and each individual was a different machine, how would the justice of heaven or even that of earth require the same effects from dissimilar machines?

If earthly justice punishes dissimilar machines equally, it is because it cannot appreciate or take account of these dissimilarities.

Ibid. - All virtue is of precept, because it is not a question of giving praiseworthy inclinations, but of preventing from committing evil deeds.

Afterword by the Translator

Diderot: The Encyclopedian of the Enlightenment and the Martyrdom of Evil

Denis Diderot was a central philosopher of the Enlightenment era who left a mark on the fields of philosophy, literature, and social thought in the Empirical tradition. Born in 1713 in Langres, France, Diderot's intellectual path was shaped by a diverse range of influences, but primarily the popular Materialist thinkers that were dominating France. He wrote novels, plays, stories, essays, dialogues, art criticism, literary criticisms and translations largely in dialogic form. He published at the same time as Adam Smith, Immanuel Kant, Rousseau and Voltaire. He drew inspiration from the Empiricist works of John Locke, Pierre Bayle, and David Hume. Diderot's own philosophy centered on the belief in human reason, the pursuit of knowledge, and the importance of freedom in society. His materialistic perspective, which emphasized the primacy of matter and the rejection of metaphysics writ large, laid the foundation for later materialist thinkers such as Karl Marx, although Marx did not think much of Diderot as he did of Bayle and Feuerbach.

Diderot was a friend of Rousseau until their falling out, a personal art critic of Catherine II, Empress of Russia, and rubbed shoulders with the giants of his day, but did not gain recognition in his lifetime. Unknown to most of his major contemporaries, distanced from the polemics of his day, and badly received by the Revolution, Diderot had to wait until the end of the nineteenth century to receive the interest and recognition of posterity in which he had placed some of his hopes. Some of his texts remained unpublished until the 21st century, and the modern edition of his complete works, begun in 1975 by the Parisian publisher Hermann, has not yet been completed. Still, he contributed to some of the greatest works of history, including Rousseau's Social Contract.

Diderot did not seek a coherent philosophical system like many others of his day apart from his Encyclopedia, but he did believe in the unity of all knowledge. In most of his philosophic works, he brings ideas together and contrasts them, which is reminiscent of Nietzsche's works. Diderot also frequently reworked his texts, and in the second half of his life even wrote a few additions (notably to the Philosophical Reflections and the Letter on the Aveugles) to reflect his own evolving thinking. Most of his works are intended to stimulate thought rather than to express his personal ideas, although he does posit fundamental metaphysical truths. Reason is Teleological in nature, and his materialism has elements of an Eschatology. In the introductions of his massive Encyclopedia, he posits a unity of knowledge which is largely materialistic, but allows room for Theology to be necessary for a healthy society, a perspective it sounds like he adopted from Voltaire:

> The physical beings act on the senses. The impressions of these Beings excite the perceptions of them in the Mind. The Understanding deals with its perceptions only in three ways, according to its three main faculties, Memory, Reason, Imagination. Where the Understanding makes a pure and simple enumeration of its perceptions by Memory; where he examines them, compares them, and digests them by Reason; where he likes to imitate them and counterfeit them by the Imagination. Whence results a general distribution of human knowledge which appears fairly well founded; in History , which relates to Memory; in Philosophy, which emanates from Reason; & in Poetry, which is born from Imagination.

> The natural progress of the human mind is to rise from individuals to species, from species to genera, from neighboring genera to distant genera, and to form at each step a Science; or at least to add a new branch to some Science already formed: thus the notion of an uncreated, infinite Intelligence, &c. that we encounter in Nature, and that sacred History announces to us; and that of a created intelligence, finite & united to a body that we perceive in man, & that we suppose in the brute, have led us to the notion of a created, finite Intelligence, which would have no body ; & from there, to the general notion of the Spirit. Further the general properties of Beings, both spiritual and corporeal, being existence,, duration , substance , attribute , &c. these properties have been examined, and the Ontology, or Science of Being in general, has been formed from them . So we had in reverse order, first Ontology; then the Science of the Spirit, or Pneumatology , or what is commonly called Particular Metaphysics : & this Science is distributed in Science of God… hence Religion & Theology proper, whence by abuse, Superstition . In the doctrine of good and evil spirits, or of angels and demons; hence Divination , & the chimera of Black Magic . Into Science of the Soul, which has been subdivided into Science of the reasonable Soul which conceives, and into Science of the sensitive Soul, which is limited to sensations.

One of Diderot's most famous contribution to history is as his role as the chief editor of the Encyclopédie, a monumental project that sought to compile and disseminate knowledge across various disciplines. He is often referred to as "the Encyclopedia". This ambitious undertaking was massive effort involving numerous contributors, and it aimed to challenge traditional authority and promote the ideals of the Enlightenment. Diderot's vision for the Encyclopédie was to create a compendium that would empower individuals to think critically and independently, fostering intellectual progress in society, similar to Voltaire's Philosophic Dictionary. It is a prime example of an Enlightenment text.

German Continental Idealism

Kant refutes the presuppositionless science of Diderot and the French Materialists, which were inspired by Kant's great enemy Hume, across many works including Metaphysical Foundations of Natural Science (Metaphysische Anfangsgründe der Naturwissenschaft). Kant and Hegel focused on their own work and rarely wrote any polemics, but Hegel does comment on Diderot in his later works. In his Lectures on Aesthetics, Hegel comments extensively on Diderot, once again exposing the supposedly non-existent Metaphysical side of Materialism and Natural Philosophy:

> What was called French philosophy, Voltaire, Montesquieu, Rousseau, d'Alembert, Diderot, and what then appeared as Enlightenment in Germany, also frowned upon as atheism, we can distinguish three sides of it: 1. its negative side, which was most resented; 2. the positive; 3. the philosophical, metaphysical.

> Among the French, Diderot in particular insisted in this sense on naturalness and imitation of the existing. Among us Germans, on the other hand, it was Goethe and Schiller who in a higher sense took a similar path in their youth, but within this lively naturalness and particularity sought deeper content and essential conflicts of interest,

> In the similar relation Goethe already says in his notes to the translation of Diderot's Versuch über die Malerei: "One by no means admits that it is easier to make a weak coloring more harmonious than a strong one; but admittedly, if the coloring is strong, if colors appear vivid, then the eye also feels harmony and disharmony much more vividly; but if one needs the colors weakened, some bright, others mixed, others soiled in the picture, then admittedly no one knows whether he sees a harmonious or disharmonious picture; but that one knows at most to say that it is ineffective, that it is insignificant."

> Diderot, Lessing, also Goethe and Schiller [Hegel knew Goethe and Schiller personally] in their youth turned in more recent times mainly to the side of real naturalness: Lessing with full education and subtlety of observation, Schiller and Goethe with preference for the immediate liveliness of uncompromised coarseness and power. That people could speak to each other as in the Greek, but mainly and the latter statement is correct in the French comedy and tragedy, was considered unnatural.

Friedrich Nietzsche, a philosopher of the 19th century, also commended Diderot's critical approach, asserting, "Diderot taught us to doubt everything." In his 1881 The Scarlet Dawn, Nietzsche comments on

"Only the lonely man is evil," cried Diderot: and immediately Rousseau felt mortally wounded [Rousseau talks about this dispute in his Confessions]. Consequently he admitted to himself that Diderot was right. In fact, every evil inclination in the midst of society and conviviality has so much compulsion to put on, so much larvae to undertake, so often to lay itself in the Procrustean bed of virtue, that one could quite well speak of a martyrdom of evil. In solitude all this falls away. He who is evil is most so in solitude: also best-and consequently, for the eye of him who sees everywhere only a spectacle, also most beautiful.

Presuppostionless Science and the Protestant Tradition of Self-Deception

Diderot's philosophy emphasized the power of reason and the importance of empirical observation, although he shunned away from clear Atheism. In his early Philosophic Questions, he writes "superstition is more unjust to God than atheism". His semi-Atheism is similar to that of Voltaire- he is really just so upset with the religious infighting and violence of the 17th century, that Atheism becomes appealing, but he never gives himself fully over to it. He writes in the same work "Someone was once asked if there were any true atheists. Do you believe," he replied, "that there are any true Christians?"

He did have a love of Empiricism. In his 1749 *Letter on the Blind*, Diderot contemplated the nature of perception and argued that sensory experience shapes our understanding of reality. He wrote, "We see only what we are able to see. Sight is a perspective sense like touch, taste, and smell." This materialism emerged later in his life, but his emphasis on morality kept him returning to the concept of beauty, which he could not bring himself to say is purely a material, epiphenomenal reality.

The materialist Sociologist Michel Foucault noted, "Diderot reminds us that philosophy should not only address metaphysical questions but also engage with the concrete realities of human existence." Marx could not agree more. The fundamental problem here, as Orwell, Solzhenitsyn and Dostoevsky reply, is that this worldview is itself a religion- the very perception of the material world is metaphysical first, so the Materialist worldview is never what it claims. Freud made this accusation about Marx and the Materialists like Diderot. Freud saw that the French and German Materialist trends were still religious in nature despite their violent claims to be purely materialistic, atheistic and pro-science:

Marx's theory I have been alienated by sentences such as that the development of social forms is a natural-historical process, or that the changes in social stratification emerge from each other on the path of a dialectical process. I am not at all sure that I understand these assertions correctly, nor do they sound "materialist," but rather like a precipitation of that dark Hegelian philosophy through whose school Marx also passed.

This was exactly what Marx accused Feuerbach of, a link in a long chain of Materialists accusing the materialists before them of not being real materialists, mimicking the infinite feuds we see in Protestantism. Jung makes this exact same accusation against Freud's repetition of Feuerbach's Materialism- Freud's entire worldview rests upon deeply held religious axioms- a Teleology. The act of science itself is a belief, utilizing a set of a priori assumptions that reality can manifest itself to consciousness in a rational fashion. Marx writes in The Holy Family:

> We need not speak of Volney, Dupuis, Diderot, etc., as little as of the Physiocrats, after we have proved the double descent of French materialism from the physics of Descartes and from English materialism, as well as the opposition of French materialism to the metaphysics of the seventeenth century, to the metaphysics of Descartes, Spinoza, Malebranche, and Leibniz. This opposition could only become visible to the Germans since they themselves stood in opposition to speculative metaphysics.

Freud argues most clearly against Platonic Ontology in his 1927 *Die Zukunft einer Illusion*, where he states that science can be ideology or metaphysics-free, i.e. Presuppositionless. Freud accused Marxism of being "darkly Hegelian", but Freud's views on history as having an intrinsic Telos, which he adopted from the metaphysician Darwin, is also deeply Hegelian. His entire Phylogenesis analysis is deeply Teleological. Nietzsche makes this observation about the Metaphysical roots of Darwinian Science, which believed to be "presuppositionless science":

> [Hegel] dared to teach that the species concepts develop apart from one another: with which sentence the minds in Europe were performed to the last great scientific movement, to Darwinism for without Hegel, no Darwin....Hegel, in particular, was its *retarder par excellence*... in his grandiose attempt he made to persuade us to the divinity of existence.

Freud, of course, somehow managed to find incest in Diderot, which he mentions in his Lectures on Psychoanalysis:

Among the writings of the encyclopedist Diderot you will find a famous dialogue Le neveu de Rameau, which was edited in German by no less a person than Goethe. There you can read the curious sentence: Si le petit sauvage était abandonné à lui-même, qu'il conservât toute son imbécillité et qu'il réunît au peu de raison de l'enfant au berceau la violence des passions de l'homme de trente ans, il tordrait le col à son père et coucherait avec sa mère." [If the little savage were left to himself, if he retained all his imbecility and combined the little reason of the child in the cradle with the violence of the passions of the man of thirty, he would wring his father's neck and sleep with his mother."]... And this is one of the motives why we have placed the study of dreams before that of neurotic symptoms.

Schopenhauer, who coined the basic constructs of the Unconscious used by Freud, found Diderot to be a useful philosopher, but one who collapse the Subject-Object paradigm with this Aristotelean materialism, thus removing the will to live. Nietzsche would develop this line of thought further. Schopenhauer notes:

Diderot already said, in Rameau's nephew, that those who teach a science are not those who understand it and practice it seriously, as they have no time to teach it. Those others live only on science: it is to them an efficient cow that supplies them with butter.

Victor Hugo comments on the French philosophers extensively, mentioning Diderot hundreds of times across his works. In Les Miserables he writes:

The encyclopedists, led by Diderot, the physiocrats, led by Turgot, the philosophers, led by Voltaire, the utopians, led by Rousseau, these are four sacred legions. The immense advance of humanity towards the light is due to them. They are the four avant-gardes of the human race going to the four cardinal points of progress, Diderot towards the beautiful, Turgot towards the useful, Voltaire towards the true, Rousseau towards the just. But, beside and below the philosophers, there were the sophists, poisonous vegetation mixed with salubrious growth, hemlock in the virgin forest. While the executioner burned on the staircase of the palace of justice the great liberating books of the century, writers today forgotten published, with the privilege of the king, one does not know which strangely disorganizing writings, avidly read by the miserable.

Rousseau, Diderot and the French Revolution

Diderot was overshadowed by the personalities of Rousseau and Voltaire. As Victor Hugo said in The Toilers of the Sea:

Is it possible to speak about Voltaire calmly and fairly? When a man dominates a century and embodies progress, he does not have to deal with criticism, but with hatred.

Goethe likewise recognized that Voltaire eclipsed the other French intellectuals of his day:

In Voltaire, the highest writer conceivable among the French, the one most in keeping with the nation. The qualities that are demanded of an intellectual man, that are admired in him, are manifold, and the demands of the French are in this respect, if not greater, yet more manifold than those of other nations. Depth, genius, perception, sublimity, nature, talent, merit, nobility, spirit, beautiful spirit, good spirit, feeling, sensibility, taste, good taste, understanding, correctness, decorum, tone, good tone, court tone, variety, abundance, richness, fruitfulness, warmth, magic, grace, gracefulness, pleasingness, lightness, vivacity, refinement, brilliant, saillantes, petillantes, piquant, delicate, ingenious, style, versification, harmony, purity, correction, elegance, perfection. Of all these qualities and expressions of mind, perhaps only the first and the last, the depth in the layout and the perfection in the execution, can be disputed to Voltairen. All that, by the way, of abilities and skills in a brilliant way fills the breadth of the world, he has possessed and thereby extended his fame over the earth.

Still, Diderot's humanistic ideas found resonance in the realm of political thought and largely coincided with Rousseau and Voltaire.. His advocacy for individual freedom and the importance of reason informed his views on governance and social organization. Diderot's political thought aligned with the ideals of the broader Enlightenment, which emphasized the rights and autonomy of individuals. His work played a significant role in shaping the ideas that would later underpin democratic societies along with Rousseau and his social contract.

Rousseau diatribes about his interactions with Diderot extensively in his 1790 Confessions. The two shared a close intellectual friendship until Rousseau broke it off due to Diderot criticizing his life choices, something Rousseau did to many friends. Eventually he broke with him for telling a secret he told him in confidence. Still, Rousseau hailed Diderot as a champion of freedom, declaring, "He has courageously battled against prejudice, fanaticism, and intolerance." Rousseau's Discourse on Inequality was one of Diderot's favorite works, and the two reviewed and improved each other's works. Rousseau writes in Confessions:

Diderot, younger than them, was about my age. He liked music, he knew the theory of it; we spoke about it together: he also spoke to me about his projects of works. This soon led to a more intimate relationship between us, which lasted fifteen years, and which would probably still last, if unfortunately, and through his fault, I had not been thrown into his same profession [Poetry]....

I loved Diderot tenderly, I esteemed him sincerely, and I counted with complete confidence on the same feelings on his part. But, fed up with his indefatigable obstinacy in eternally antagonizing me about my tastes, my inclinations, my way of life, about everything that interested only me; revolted to see a man younger than me wanting to govern me at all costs like a child; repulsed by his ease in promising, annoyed by so many appointments given and missed on his part, and by his fantasy of always giving new ones, to miss them again; embarrassed to wait for him uselessly three or four times a month, on days marked by himself, and to dine alone in the evening, after having gone to meet him as far as Saint-Denis, and having waited for him all day: my heart was already full of his many wrongs...

This last trait decided me; and, resolved to break with Diderot forever, I deliberated only on the manner; for I had realized that secret breaks turned to my detriment, in that they left the mask of friendship to my most cruel enemies.

Unlike Rousseau, Diderot lived a respectable family life, and was missed by his community. We read in We read in Grimm's Correspondence, March 1771:

"M. Diderot, master cutler in Langres, died in 1759, generally missed in his town, leaving his children an honest fortune for his state, and a reputation for virtue and probity desirable in any state. I saw him three months before his death. On my way to Geneva in March 1759, I passed through Langres on purpose, and I shall be proud all my life to have known this respectable old man.

He left three children: an eldest son, Denis Diderot, born in 1713, our philosopher; a daughter of excellent heart and uncommon firmness of character, who, from the moment of her mother's death, devoted herself entirely to the service of her father and his house, and for this reason refused to marry; a youngest son who sided with the Church: he is a canon of the cathedral church of Langres and one of the great saints of the diocese. He is a man of strange mind, of outrageous devotion, and in whom I have little faith in right ideas or feelings. The father loved his eldest son out of inclination and passion; his daughter, out of gratitude and tenderness; and his youngest son, out of reflection and respect for the state he had embraced. "

Goethe, Schiller and the Impetuous of the Romantic Era

In the field of literature, Diderot's belief in the power of storytelling and his emphasis on portraying the complexity of human nature can be seen in his novel, "Jacques the Fatalist." Through this work, Diderot explores the themes of determinism and free will, a religious theme he wrestles with due to his interest in Materialism, but his dedication to and recognition of the importance of morality.

Schiller and Goethe spoke of Diderot frequently, and Goethe introduced the German-speaking world to his works. Some of his works have been lost in French, but we have German translations thanks to Goethe. Goethe's play The Natural Daughter may have been based on Diderot's The Natural Son. In his letters, Goethe displays an incredible understanding of Diderot, and an appreciation of his Aesthetics:

> On the other hand, I came across Diderot yesterday, who delighted me and moved my innermost thoughts. Almost every dictum is a spark of light that illuminates the secrets of art, and his remarks are so much from the highest and innermost of art that they also dominate everything that is only related to it and are just as much pointers for the poet as for the painter. If the writing does not belong to you yourself, that I can keep it longer and get it again, then I will prescribe it to myself.

> Since I happened to come across the Diderot first, I have not yet moved on to the Staelische Schrift; however, both works are now quite a mental necessity for me, because my own work, in which I live and must live completely, limits my circle so much.

> You can keep Diderot longer; it is a wonderful book and speaks almost more to the poet than to the visual artist, although it often shines before the latter with a powerful torch.

> It seems to me that Diderot is like many others who hit the truth with their sensibility, but sometimes lose it again through raison d'être. In aesthetic works, he still looks far too much at extraneous and moral purposes; he does not look for them enough in the object and in its representation. The beautiful work of art must always serve something else for him. And since the truly beautiful and perfect in art necessarily improves man, he seeks this effect of art in its content and in a certain result for the intellect, or for moral feeling. I believe it is one of the advantages of our newer philosophy that we have a pure formula to express the subjective effect of the aesthetic without destroying its character.

Tim Newcomb
Stuttgart, Germany
Summer 2023

Timeline of Diderot's Life & Works

1713
Denis Diderot is born on October 5th in Langres, France.

1732
Diderot enters the Collège d'Harcourt in Paris to study philosophy and theology.

The same year, Jean-Jacques Rousseau is born, who will become a key figure in the Enlightenment and a friend of Diderot

1746
Diderot begins contributing to the Encyclopédie, one of his most significant works, serving as its chief editor until 1772.

1759
Diderot publishes "Letter on the Blind for the Use of Those Who See," where he explores philosophical ideas about perception and knowledge.

Adam Smith publishes "The Theory of Moral Sentiments," an influential work on ethics and economics.

1762
Diderot publishes "Supplement to Bougainville's Voyage," which criticizes colonialism and advocates for the rights of indigenous peoples.

Jean-Jacques Rousseau publishes "The Social Contract," a significant work on political philosophy which Diderot contributed to.

1770
Diderot publishes "Thoughts on Interpretation," which discusses morality, virtue, and the importance of empathy.

Immanuel Kant publishes "Critique of Pure Reason," a groundbreaking work on epistemology and metaphysics.

1773
Diderot is briefly imprisoned for his controversial writings, causing him to face censorship and restrictions. Rousseau describes this whole ordeal in his Confessions.

1784
Diderot's "D'Alembert's Dream" is published posthumously, reflecting his ideas on materialism, atheism, and determinism.

Immanuel Kant publishes "Groundwork of the Metaphysics of Morals"

1784
Denis Diderot dies at 71 years old on July 31st in Paris, leaving behind a legacy as a

prominent figure of the Enlightenment and a champion of intellectual freedom. The French Revolution looms on the horizon, marking a significant turning point in European history.

1791

The last volume of the Encyclopédie is published, solidifying Diderot's contribution to the dissemination of knowledge and the advancement of Enlightenment ideals.

1792

The French Revolution is fully underway, fueled by the ideas of liberty, equality, and fraternity, taking Voltaire and Rousseau as their champions, while Diderot's contributions are largely relegated to history.

Glossary of Philosophic Terminology in Diderot

Enlightenment (Lumières)

The Enlightenment refers to an intellectual and cultural movement in the 17th and 18th centuries that emphasized reason, science, and skepticism towards traditional authority. It is generally said to have begun in the late 17th century, and Diderot lived through the heart of it, a contemporary of Voltaire and Goethe. Denis Diderot's life and works unfold against the backdrop of the Enlightenment, witnessing the rise of influential thinkers like Rousseau, Adam Smith, and Kant.

"Dare to know! Have courage to use your own reason!" From "What is Enlightenment?"

Materialism (Matérialisme)

Materialism is the philosophical belief that the fundamental constituents of reality are physical matter and energy, and that consciousness and thought are byproducts of material interactions. In other works, it is Anti-Metaphysical, claiming all reality is material and nothing is super-rational. Knowledge is purely observation.

"All things in the universe are material, and everything is brought about by material causes." *D'Alembert's Dream*

Determinism (Déterminisme)

Determinism is the philosophical doctrine that every event, including human actions, is ultimately determined by external causes and cannot be otherwise.

"Nature never turns aside from the laws of motion." *System of Nature*

Atheism (Athéisme)

Atheism is the disbelief or rejection of the existence of deities or gods, which Diderot entertains but does not fully give himself over to.

"I do not believe in the existence of a God; his existence is impossible, and I am convinced of the impossibility." *D'Alembert's Dream*

Skepticism (Scepticisme)

Skepticism is the philosophical position that doubts or suspends judgment regarding claims to knowledge, asserting that absolute certainty is not attainable.

"There are no true miracles, just facts that defy our understanding." *Philosophical Thoughts*

Empiricism (Empirisme)

Empiricism is the theory that all knowledge is derived from sensory experience and observation, an idea which Kant spent most of his life dismantling.

"Observation is the foundation of all knowledge, and experiment is the guide." *Supplement to Bougainville's Voyage*

Morality (Morale)

Morality refers to the principles or rules of right conduct and ethical judgment concerning what is right and wrong.

"Virtue consists in doing good to others, but what good is it if we do not know how to do it?"
Thoughts on Interpretation

Liberty (Liberté)

Liberty is the state of being free from oppression or arbitrary restrictions, allowing individuals to exercise their rights and autonomy.

"Man is born free, and everywhere he is in chains."
Letter on the Blind for the Use of Those Who See and Rousseau's Social Contract

Social Contract (Contrat social)

Diderot discussed the social contract with Rousseau, who is historically known as the founder of the idea. The social contract is a hypothetical agreement among individuals forming a society, where they voluntarily give up certain freedoms in exchange for security and the benefits of collective living. Diderot commented on and helped Rousseau write his major publication on the idea.

"The sovereign is formed by the union of all the individuals who make up the social body."
On the Social Contract

Enlightenment Despotism (Despotisme éclairé)

Enlightenment despotism refers to a system of government in which an absolute monarch or ruler exercises power with the goal of implementing Enlightenment ideals and reforms.

"I am obliged to be a despot in order to achieve great things for humanity."
letter to Catherine the Great

Printed in Great Britain
by Amazon